GLEANINGS IN BUDDHA-FIELDS
Studies of Hand and Soul in the Far East

GLEANINGS IN BUDDHA-FIELDS

STUDIES OF HAND AND SOUL
IN THE FAR EAST

by LAFCADIO HEARN

CHARLES E. TUTTLE COMPANY
Rutland, Vermont & Tokyo, Japan

Representatives
Continental Europe: BOXERBOOKS, INC., *Zurich*
British Isles: PRENTICE-HALL INTERNATIONAL, INC., *London*
Australasia: PAUL FLESCH & CO., PTY. LTD., *Melbourne*
Canada: M. G. HURTIG LTD., *Edmonton*

Published by the Charles E. Tuttle Company, Inc.
of Rutland, Vermont & Tokyo, Japan
with editorial offices at
Suido 1-chome, 2-6, Bunkyo-ku, Tokyo, Japan

© *1971, by Charles E. Tuttle Co., Inc.*

All rights reserved

Library of Congress Catalog Card No. 72-146523

International Standard Book No. 0-8048-0978-X

First edition published 1897 by Houghton, Mifflin, and Co., Boston
First Tuttle edition published 1971
Second printing, 1972

0293-000277-4615
PRINTED IN JAPAN

TABLE OF CONTENTS

		PAGE
	Publisher's Foreword	vii
I.	A Living God	1
II.	Out of the Street	29
III.	Notes of a Trip to Kyōto	43
IV.	Dust	84
V.	About Faces in Japanese Art	97
VI.	Ningyō-no-Haka	124
VII.	In Ōsaka	132
VIII.	Buddhist Allusions in Japanese Folk-Song	185
IX.	Nirvana	211
X.	The Rebirth of Katsugorō	267
XI.	Within the Circle	291

PUBLISHER'S FOREWORD

LAFCADIO HEARN is almost as Japanese as haiku. Both are an art form, an institution in Japan. Haiku is indigenous to the nation; Hearn became a Japanese citizen and married a Japanese, taking the name Yakumo Koizumi. His flight from Western materialism brought him to Japan in 1890. His search for beauty and tranquility, for pleasing customs and lasting values, kept him there the rest of his life, a confirmed Japanophile. He became the great interpreter of things Japanese to the West. His keen intellect, poetic imagination, and wonderfully clear style permitted him to penetrate to the very essence of things Japanese.

In *Gleanings In Buddha-Fields*, Hearn discusses the Buddhist theory of the nature of pleasure, concluding that Japanese popular pleasures have the peculiarity of being evanescent and complex—and amazingly cheap. But for the latter factor, the race could not have discovered the secret of making pleasure the commonest instead of the costliest of experiences—the divine art of creating the beautiful out of nothing! One explanation for this is the capacity of the people to find in everything natural—in landscapes, mists, clouds, sunsets; in the sight of birds, insects and flowers—a much keener pleasure than Westerners do, as the vividness of their artistic presentations of visual experience bears witness.

This engaging and enlightening book is of no less value today than it was when it made its first appearance in 1897. Then, as now, there was an insatiable Western interest in Japan, which had only recently emerged into the modern world. For the present-day reader the impressions and opinions of earlier Western writers on Japan still retain a remarkable validity, and those of Lafcadio Hearn are among the most enduring in this respect. It is therefore both a privilege and a pleasure to bring back into print this attractive example of his work.

GLEANINGS IN BUDDHA-FIELDS

I

A LIVING GOD

I

Of whatever dimension, the temples or shrines of pure Shintō are all built in the same archaic style. The typical shrine is a windowless oblong building of unpainted timber, with a very steep overhanging roof; the front is the gable end; and the upper part of the perpetually closed doors is wooden lattice-work, — usually a grating of bars closely set and crossing each other at right angles. In most cases the structure is raised slightly above the ground on wooden pillars; and the queer peaked façade, with its visor-like apertures and the fantastic projections of beam-work above its gable-angle, might remind the European traveler of certain old Gothic forms of dormer. There is no artificial color. The plain wood [1] soon turns, under the action of rain and sun, to a natural grey, varying according to surface exposure from the silvery tone of birch bark to the sombre grey of basalt. So shaped and so tinted, the isolated country *yashiro* may seem less like a work of joinery than a feature of the scenery, — a rural form related to nature as closely as rocks and trees, — a something that came into existence only as a manifestation of Ohotsuchi-no-Kami, the Earth-god, the primeval divinity of the land.

Why certain architectural forms produce in the beholder a feeling of weirdness is a question about which I should like to theorize some day: at present I shall venture only to say that Shintō shrines evoke such a feeling. It grows with familiarity instead of weakening; and a knowledge of popular beliefs is apt to intensify it. We have no English words by which these queer shapes can be sufficiently described, — much less any language able to communicate the peculiar impression which they make. Those Shintō terms which we loosely render by the words "temple" and "shrine" are really untrans-

[1] Usually *hinoki* (*Chamæcyparis obtusa*).

latable; — I mean that the Japanese ideas attaching to them cannot be conveyed by translation. The so-called "august house" of the Kami is not so much a temple, in the classic meaning of the term, as it is a haunted room, a spirit-chamber, a ghost-house; many of the lesser divinities being veritably ghosts, — ghosts of great warriors and heroes and rulers and teachers, who lived and loved and died hundreds or thousands of years ago. I fancy that to the Western mind the word "ghost-house" will convey, better than such terms as "shrine" and "temple," some vague notion of the strange character of the Shintō *miya* or *yashiro*, — containing in its perpetual dusk nothing more substantial than symbols or tokens, the latter probably of paper. Now the emptiness behind the visored front is more suggestive than anything material could possibly be; and when you remember that millions of people during thousands of years have worshiped their great dead before such *yashiro*, — that a whole race still believes those buildings tenanted by viewless conscious personalities, — you are apt also to reflect how difficult it would be to prove the faith absurd. Nay! in spite of Occidental reluctances, — in spite of whatever you may think it expedient to say or not to say at a later time about the experience, — you may very likely find yourself for a moment forced into the attitude of respect toward possibilities. Mere cold reasoning will not help you far in the opposite direction. The evidence of the senses counts for little: you know there are ever so many realities which can neither be seen nor heard nor felt, but which exist as forces, — tremendous forces. Then again you cannot mock the conviction of forty millions of people while that conviction thrills all about you like the air, — while conscious that it is pressing upon your psychical being just as the atmosphere presses upon your physical being. As for myself, whenever I am alone in the presence of a Shintō shrine, I have the sensation of being haunted; and I cannot help thinking about the possible apperceptions of the haunter. And this tempts me to fancy how I should feel if I myself were a god, — dwelling in some old Izumo shrine on the summit of a hill, guarded by stone lions and shadowed by a holy grove.

Elfishly small my habitation might be, but never too small, because I should have neither size nor form. I should be only a vibration, — a motion invisible as of ether or of magnetism; though able sometimes to shape me a shadow-body, in the likeness of my former visible self, when I should wish to make apparition.

As air to the bird, as water to the fish, so would all substance be permeable to the essence of me. I should pass at will through the walls of my dwelling to swim in the long gold bath of a sunbeam, to thrill in the heart of a flower, to ride on the neck of a dragon-fly.

Power above life and power over death would be mine, — and the power of self-extension, and the power of self-multiplication, and the power of being in all places at one and the same moment. Simultaneously in a hundred homes I should hear myself worshiped, I should inhale the vapor of a hundred offerings: each evening, from my place within a hundred household shrines, I should see the holy lights lighted for me in lamplets of red clay, in lamplets of brass, — the lights of the

Kami, kindled with purest fire and fed with purest oil.

But in my yashiro upon the hill I should have greatest honor: there betimes I should gather the multitude of my selves together; there should I unify my powers to answer supplication.

From the dusk of my ghost-house I should look for the coming of sandaled feet, and watch brown supple fingers weaving to my bars the knotted papers which are records of vows, and observe the motion of the lips of my worshipers making prayer: —

— "*Harai-tamai kiyomé-tamaé!* . . . We have beaten drums, we have lighted fires; yet the land thirsts and the rice fails. Deign out of thy divine pity to give us rain, O Daimyō-jin!"

— "*Harai - tamai kiyomé -tamaé!* . . . I am dark, too dark, because I have toiled in the field, because the sun hath looked upon me. Deign thou augustly to make me white, very white, — white like the women of the city, O Daimyōjin!"

— "*Harai-tamai kiyomé-tamaé!* . . . For Tsukamoto Motokichi our son, a soldier of twenty-nine: that he may conquer and come back quickly to us, — soon, very soon, — we humbly supplicate, O Daimyōjin!"

Sometimes a girl would whisper all her heart to me: "Maiden of eighteen years, I am loved by a youth of twenty. He is good; he is true; but poverty is with us, and the path of our love is dark. Aid us with thy great divine pity! — help us that we may become united, O Daimyōjin!" Then to the bars of my shrine she would hang a thick soft tress of hair, — her own hair, glossy and black as the wing of the crow, and bound with a cord of mulberry-paper. And in the fragrance of that offering, — the simple fragrance of her peasant youth, — I, the ghost and god, should find again the feelings of the years when I was man and lover.

Mothers would bring their children to my threshold, and teach them to revere me, saying, "Bow down before the great bright God; make homage to the Daimyōjin." Then I should hear the fresh soft clapping of little hands, and remember that I, the ghost and god, had been a father.

Daily I should hear the plash of pure cool water poured out for me, and the tinkle of thrown coin, and the pattering of dry rice into my wooden box, like a pattering of rain; and I should be refreshed by the spirit of the water, and strengthened by the spirit of the rice.

Festivals would be held to honor me. Priests, black-coiffed and linen-vestured, would bring me offerings of fruits and fish and seaweed and rice-cakes and rice-wine, — masking their faces with sheets of white paper, so as not to breathe upon my food. And the *miko* their daughters, fair girls in crimson *hakama* and robes of snowy white, would come to dance with tinkling of little bells, with waving of silken fans, that I might be gladdened by the bloom of their youth, that I might delight in the charm of their grace. And there would be music of many thousand years ago, — weird music of drums and flutes, — and songs in a tongue no longer spoken; while the miko, the darlings of the gods, would poise and pose before me: —

... "*Whose virgins are these, — the virgins who stand like flowers before the Deity? They are the virgins of the august Deity.*

"*The august music, the dancing of the virgins, — the Deity will be pleased to hear, the Deity will rejoice to see.*

"*Before the great bright God the virgins dance, — the virgins all like flowers newly opened.*" . . .

Votive gifts of many kinds I should be given: painted paper lanterns bearing my sacred name, and towels of divers colors printed with the number of the years of the giver, and pictures commemorating the fulfillment of prayers for the healing of sickness, the saving of ships, the quenching of fire, the birth of sons.

Also my Karashishi, my guardian lions, would be honored. I should see my pilgrims tying sandals of straw to their necks and to their paws, with prayer to the Karashishi-Sama for strength of foot.

I should see fine moss, like emerald fur, growing slowly, slowly, upon the backs of those lions; — I should see the sprouting of lichens upon their flanks and upon their shoulders, in specklings of dead-silver, in patches of dead-gold; — I should watch, through years of generations, the gradual sideward sinking of their pedestals undermined by frost and rain, until at last my lions would lose their balance, and fall, and break their mossy heads off. After which the people would give me new lions of another form, — lions of granite or of bronze, with gilded teeth and gilded eyes, and tails like a torment of fire.

Between the trunks of the cedars and pines, between the jointed columns of the bamboos, I should observe, season after season, the changes of the colors of the valley: the falling of the snow of winter and the falling of the snow of cherry-flowers; the lilac spread of the *miyakobana;* the blazing yellow of the *natané;* the sky-blue mirrored in flooded levels, — levels dotted with the moon-shaped hats of the toiling people who would love me; and at last the pure and tender green of the growing rice.

The *muku*-birds and the *uguisu* would fill the shadows of my grove with ripplings and

A LIVING GOD

purlings of melody; — the bell-insects, the crickets, and the seven marvelous cicadæ of summer would make all the wood of my ghost-house thrill to their musical storms. Betimes I should enter, like an ecstasy, into the tiny lives of them, to quicken the joy of their clamor, to magnify the sonority of their song.

But I never can become a god, — for this is the nineteenth century; and nobody can be really aware of the nature of the sensations of a god — unless there be gods in the flesh. Are there? Perhaps — in very remote districts — one or two. There used to be living gods.

Anciently any man who did something extraordinarily great or good or wise or brave might be declared a god after his death, no matter how humble his condition in life. Also good people who had suffered great cruelty and injustice might be apotheosized; and there still survives the popular inclination to pay posthumous honor and to make prayer to the spirits of those who die voluntary deaths under particular circumstances, — to souls of unhappy lovers, for example. (Probably the old customs which made this tendency had their origin in the wish to appease the vexed spirit, although to-day the experience of great suffering seems to be thought of as qualifying its possessor for divine conditions of being; — and there would be no foolishness whatever in such a thought.) But there were even more remarkable deifications. Certain persons, while still alive, were honored by having temples built for their spirits, and were treated as gods; not, indeed, as national gods, but as lesser divinities, — tutelar deities, perhaps, or village-gods. There was, for instance, Hamaguchi Gohei, a farmer of the district of Arita in the province of Kishu, who was made a god before he died. And I think he deserved it.

II

Before telling the story of Hamaguchi Gohei, I must say a few words about certain laws — or, more correctly speaking, customs having all the force of laws — by which many village communities were ruled in pre-Meiji times. These customs were based upon the social experience of ages; and though they differed in minor details according to province or district, their main signification was every where about the same. Some were ethical, some industrial, some religious; and all matters were regulated by them, — even individual behavior. They preserved peace, and they compelled mutual help and mutual kindness. Sometimes there might be serious fighting between different villages, — little peasant wars about questions of water supply or boundaries; but quarreling between men of the same community could not be tolerated in an age of vendetta, and the whole village would resent any needless disturbance of the internal peace. To some degree this state of things still exists in the more old-fashioned provinces: the people know how to live without quarreling, not to say fighting. Anywhere, as a general rule, Japanese fight only to kill; and when a sober man goes so far as to strike a blow, he virtually rejects communal protection, and takes his life into his own hands with every probability of losing it.

The private conduct of the other sex was regulated by some remarkable obligations entirely outside of written codes. A peasant girl, before marriage, enjoyed far more liberty than was permitted to city girls. She might be known to have a lover; and unless her parents objected very strongly, no blame would be given to her: it was regarded as an honest union, — honest, at least, as to intention. But having once made a choice, the girl was held bound by that choice. If it were discovered that she met another admirer secretly, the people would strip her naked, allowing her only a *shuro*-leaf for apron, and drive her in mockery through every street and alley of the village. During this public disgrace of their daughter, the parents of the girl dared not show their faces abroad; they were expected to share her shame, and they had to remain in their house, with all the shutters fastened up. Afterward the girl was sentenced to banishment for five years. But at the end of that period she was considered to have expiated her fault, and she could return home with the certainty of being spared further reproaches.

The obligation of mutual help in time of calamity or danger was the most imperative of all communal obligations. In case of fire, especially, everybody was required to give

A LIVING GOD 15

immediate aid to the best of his or her ability. Even children were not exempted from this duty. In towns and cities, of course, things were differently ordered; but in any little country village the universal duty was very plain and simple, and its neglect would have been considered unpardonable.

A curious fact is that this obligation of mutual help extended to religious matters: everybody was expected to invoke the help of the gods for the sick or the unfortunate, whenever asked to do so. For example, the village might be ordered to make a *sendo-mairi*[1] on behalf of some one seriously ill. On such occasions the Kumi-chō (each Kumi-chō was responsible for the conduct of five or more families) would run from house to house crying, "Such and such a one is very sick:

---

[1] To perform a *sendo-mairi* means to make one thousand visits to a temple, and to repeat one thousand invocations to the deity. But it is considered necessary only to go from the gate or the torii of the temple-court to the place of prayer, and back, one thousand times, repeating the invocation each time; and the task may be divided among any number of persons, — ten visits by one hundred persons, for instance, being quite as efficacious as a thousand visits by a single person.

kindly hasten all to make a sendo-mairi!"
Thereupon, however occupied at the moment, every soul in the settlement was expected to hurry to the temple, — taking care not to trip or stumble on the way, as a single misstep during the performance of a sendo-mairi was believed to mean misfortune for the sick. . . .

III

Now concerning Hamaguchi.

From immemorial time the shores of Japan have been swept, at irregular intervals of centuries, by enormous tidal waves, — tidal waves caused by earthquakes or by submarine volcanic action. These awful sudden risings of the sea are called by the Japanese *tsunami*. The last one occurred on the evening of June 17, 1896, when a wave nearly two hundred miles long struck the northeastern provinces of Miyagi, Iwaté, and Aomori, wrecking scores of towns and villages, ruining whole districts, and destroying nearly thirty thousand human lives. The story of Hamaguchi Gohei is the story of a like calamity which happened long before the era of Meiji, on another part of the Japanese coast.

A LIVING GOD

He was an old man at the time of the occurrence that made him famous. He was the most influential resident of the village to which he belonged: he had been for many years its *muraosa*, or headman; and he was not less liked than respected. The people usually called him *Ojiisan*, which means Grandfather; but, being the richest member of the community, he was sometimes officially referred to as the Chōja. He used to advise the smaller farmers about their interests, to arbitrate their disputes, to advance them money at need, and to dispose of their rice for them on the best terms possible.

Hamaguchi's big thatched farmhouse stood at the verge of a small plateau overlooking a bay. The plateau, mostly devoted to rice culture, was hemmed in on three sides by thickly wooded summits. From its outer verge the land sloped down in a huge green concavity, as if scooped out, to the edge of the water; and the whole of this slope, some three quarters of a mile long, was so terraced as to look, when viewed from the open sea, like an enormous flight of green steps, divided in the centre by a narrow white zigzag, — a streak of mountain road. Ninety thatched dwellings and a Shintō temple, composing the village proper, stood along the curve of the bay; and other houses climbed straggling up the slope for some distance on either side of the narrow road leading to the Chōja's home.

One autumn evening Hamaguchi Gohei was looking down from the balcony of his house at some preparations for a merry-making in the village below. There had been a very fine rice-crop, and the peasants were going to celebrate their harvest by a dance in the court of the *ujigami*.[1] The old man could see the festival banners (*nobori*) fluttering above the roofs of the solitary street, the strings of paper lanterns festooned between bamboo poles, the decorations of the shrine, and the brightly colored gathering of the young people. He had nobody with him that evening but his little grandson, a lad of ten; the rest of the household having gone early to the village. He would have accompanied them had he not been feeling less strong than usual.

The day had been oppressive; and in spite of a rising breeze there was still in the air

[1] Shintō parish temple.

A LIVING GOD

that sort of heavy heat which, according to the experience of the Japanese peasant, at certain seasons precedes an earthquake. And presently an earthquake came. It was not strong enough to frighten anybody; but Hamaguchi, who had felt hundreds of shocks in his time, thought it was queer, — a long, slow, spongy motion. Probably it was but the after-tremor of some immense seismic action very far away. The house crackled and rocked gently several times; then all became still again.

As the quaking ceased Hamaguchi's keen old eyes were anxiously turned toward the village. It often happens that the attention of a person gazing fixedly at a particular spot or object is suddenly diverted by the sense of something not knowingly seen at all, — by a mere vague feeling of the unfamiliar in that dim outer circle of unconscious perception which lies beyond the field of clear vision. Thus it chanced that Hamaguchi became aware of something unusual in the offing. He rose to his feet, and looked at the sea. It had darkened quite suddenly, and it was acting strangely. It seemed to be moving against the wind. *It was running away from the land.*

Within a very little time the whole village had noticed the phenomenon. Apparently no one had felt the previous motion of the ground, but all were evidently astounded by the movement of the water. They were running to the beach, and even beyond the beach, to watch it. No such ebb had been witnessed on that coast within the memory of living man. Things never seen before were making apparition; unfamiliar spaces of ribbed sand and reaches of weed-hung rock were left bare even as Hamaguchi gazed. And none of the people below appeared to guess what that monstrous ebb signified.

Hamaguchi Gohei himself had never seen such a thing before; but he remembered things told him in his childhood by his father's father, and he knew all the traditions of the coast. He understood what the sea was going to do. Perhaps he thought of the time needed to send a message to the village, or to get the priests of the Buddhist temple on the hill to sound their big bell. . . . But it would take very much longer to tell what he might have thought than it took him to think. He simply called to his grandson: —

"Tada! — quick, — very quick! . . . Light me a torch."

Taimatsu, or pine-torches, are kept in many coast dwellings for use on stormy nights, and also for use at certain Shintō festivals. The child kindled a torch at once; and the old man hurried with it to the fields, where hundreds of rice-stacks, representing most of his invested capital, stood awaiting transportation. Approaching those nearest the verge of the slope, he began to apply the torch to them, — hurrying from one to another as quickly as his aged limbs could carry him. The sun-dried stalks caught like tinder; the strengthening sea-breeze blew the blaze landward; and presently, rank behind rank, the stacks burst into flame, sending skyward columns of smoke that met and mingled into one enormous cloudy whirl. Tada, astonished and terrified, ran after his grandfather, crying, —

"Ojiisan! why? Ojiisan! why? — why?"

But Hamaguchi did not answer: he had no time to explain; he was thinking only of the four hundred lives in peril. For a while the child stared wildly at the blazing rice; then burst into tears, and ran back to the house, feeling sure that his grandfather had gone mad. Hamaguchi went on firing stack after stack, till he had reached the limit of his field; then he threw down his torch, and waited. The acolyte of the hill-temple, observing the blaze, set the big bell booming; and the people responded to the double appeal. Hamaguchi watched them hurrying in from the sands and over the beach and up from the village, like a swarming of ants, and, to his anxious eyes, scarcely faster; for the moments seemed terribly long to him. The sun was going down; the wrinkled bed of the bay, and a vast sallow speckled expanse beyond it, lay naked to the last orange glow; and still the sea was fleeing toward the horizon.

Really, however, Hamaguchi did not have very long to wait before the first party of succor arrived, — a score of agile young peasants, who wanted to attack the fire at once. But the Chōja, holding out both arms, stopped them.

"Let it burn, lads!" he commanded, — "let it be! I want the whole *mura* here. There is a great danger, — *taihen da!*"

The whole village was coming; and Hamaguchi counted. All the young men and boys were soon on the spot, and not a few of the more active women and girls; then came most of the older folk, and mothers with babies at their backs, and even children,— for children could help to pass water; and the elders too feeble to keep up with the first rush could be seen well on their way up the steep ascent. The growing multitude, still knowing nothing, looked alternately, in sorrowful wonder, at the flaming fields and at the impassive face of their Chōja. And the sun went down.

"Grandfather is mad,—I am afraid of him!" sobbed Tada, in answer to a number of questions. "He is mad. He set fire to the rice on purpose: I saw him do it!"

"As for the rice," cried Hamaguchi, "the child tells the truth. I set fire to the rice. . . . Are all the people here?"

The Kumi-chō and the heads of families looked about them, and down the hill, and made reply: "All are here, or very soon will be. . . . We cannot understand this thing."

"*Kita!*" shouted the old man at the top

of his voice, pointing to the open. "Say now if I be mad!"

Through the twilight eastward all looked, and saw at the edge of the dusky horizon a long, lean, dim line like the shadowing of a coast where no coast ever was, — a line that thickened as they gazed, that broadened as a coast-line broadens to the eyes of one approaching it, yet incomparably more quickly. For that long darkness was the returning sea, towering like a cliff, and coursing more swiftly than the kite flies.

"*Tsunami!*" shrieked the people; and then all shrieks and all sounds and all power to hear sounds were annihilated by a nameless shock heavier than any thunder, as the colossal swell smote the shore with a weight that sent a shudder through the hills, and with a foam-burst like a blaze of sheet-lightning. Then for an instant nothing was visible but a storm of spray rushing up the slope like a cloud; and the people scattered back in panic from the mere menace of it. When they looked again, they saw a white horror of sea raving over the place of their homes. It drew back roaring, and tearing out the bowels of the land as it went. Twice, thrice, five times the sea struck and ebbed, but each time with lesser surges: then it returned to its ancient bed and stayed, — still raging, as after a typhoon.

On the plateau for a time there was no word spoken. All stared speechlessly at the desolation beneath, — the ghastliness of hurled rock and naked riven cliff, the bewilderment of scooped-up deep-sea wrack and shingle shot over the empty site of dwelling and temple. The village was not; the greater part of the fields were not; even the terraces had ceased to exist; and of all the homes that had been about the bay there remained nothing recognizable except two straw roofs tossing madly in the offing. The after-terror of the death escaped and the stupefaction of the general loss kept all lips dumb, until the voice of Hamaguchi was heard again, observing gently, —

"*That was why I set fire to the rice.*"

He, their Chōja, now stood among them almost as poor as the poorest; for his wealth was gone — but he had saved four hundred lives by the sacrifice. Little Tada ran to him, and caught his hand, and asked forgiveness for having said naughty things. Whereupon the people woke up to the knowledge of why they were alive, and began to wonder at the simple, unselfish foresight that had saved them; and the headmen prostrated themselves in the dust before Hamaguchi Gohei, and the people after them.

Then the old man wept a little, partly because he was happy, and partly because he was aged and weak and had been sorely tried.

"My house remains," he said, as soon as he could find words, automatically caressing Tada's brown cheeks; "and there is room for many. Also the temple on the hill stands; and there is shelter there for the others."

Then he led the way to his house; and the people cried and shouted.

The period of distress was long, because in those days there were no means of quick communication between district and district, and the help needed had to be sent from far away. But when better times came, the people did not forget their debt to Hamaguchi Gohei. They could not make him rich; nor would he have suffered them to do so, even had it been possible. Moreover, gifts could never have sufficed as an expression of their reverential feeling towards him; for they believed that the ghost within him was divine. So they declared him a god, and thereafter called him Hamaguchi DAIMYŌJIN, thinking they could give him no greater honor; — and truly no greater honor in any country could be given to mortal man. And when they rebuilt the village, they built a temple to the spirit of him, and fixed above the front of it a tablet bearing his name in Chinese text of gold; and they worshiped him there, with prayer and with offerings. How he felt about it I cannot say; — I know only that he continued to live in his old thatched home upon the hill, with his children and his children's children, just as humanly and simply as before, while his soul was being worshiped in the shrine below. A hundred years and more he has been dead; but his temple, they tell me, still stands, and the people still pray to the ghost of the good old farmer to help them in time of fear or trouble.

o · · · · · · · o

I asked a Japanese philosopher and friend to explain to me how the peasants could rationally imagine the spirit of Hamaguchi in one place while his living body was in another. Also I inquired whether it was only one of his souls which they had worshiped during his life, and whether they imagined that particular soul to have detached itself from the rest to receive homage.

"The peasants," my friend answered, "think of the mind or spirit of a person as something which, even during life, can be in many places at the same instant. . . . Such an idea is, of course, quite different from Western ideas about the soul."

"Any more rational?" I mischievously asked.

"Well," he responded, with a Buddhist smile, "if we accept the doctrine of the unity of all mind, the idea of the Japanese peasant would appear to contain at least some adumbration of truth. I could not say so much for your Western notions about the soul."

II

OUT OF THE STREET

I

"THESE," said Manyemon, putting on the table a roll of wonderfully written Japanese manuscript, "are Vulgar Songs. If they are to be spoken of in some honorable book, perhaps it will be good to say that they are Vulgar, so that Western people may not be deceived."

Next to my house there is a vacant lot, where washermen (*sentakuya*) work in the ancient manner, — singing as they work, and whipping the wet garments upon big flat stones. Every morning at daybreak their singing wakens me; and I like to listen to it, though I cannot often catch the words. It is full of long, queer, plaintive modulations. Yesterday, the apprentice — a lad of fifteen — and the master of the washermen were singing alternately, as if answering each other; the contrast between the tones of the man, sonorous as if boomed through a conch, and the clarion alto of the boy, being very pleasant to hear. Whereupon I called Manyemon and asked him what the singing was about.

"The song of the boy," he said, "is an old song: —

> *Things never changed since the Time of the Gods:*
> *The flowing of water, the Way of Love.*

I heard it often when I was myself a boy."

"And the other song?"

"The other song is probably new: —

> *Three years thought of her,*
> *Five years sought for her;*
> *Only for one night held her in my arms.*

A very foolish song!"

"I don't know," I said. "There are famous Western romances containing nothing wiser. And what is the rest of the song?"

"There is no more: that is the whole of the song. If it be honorably desired, I can write down the songs of the washermen, and the songs which are sung in this street by the smiths and the carpenters and the bamboo-weavers and the rice-cleaners. But they are all nearly the same."

Thus came it to pass that Manyemon made for me a collection of Vulgar Songs.

By "vulgar" Manyemon meant written in the speech of the common people. He is himself an adept at classical verse, and despises the *hayari-uta*, or ditties of the day; it requires something very delicate to please him. And what pleases him I am not qualified to write about; for one must be a very good Japanese scholar to meddle with the superior varieties of Japanese poetry. If you care to know how difficult the subject is, just study the chapter on prosody in Aston's Grammar of the Japanese Written Language, or the introduction to Professor Chamberlain's Classical Poetry of the Japanese. Her poetry is the one original art which Japan has certainly not borrowed either from China or from any other country; and its most refined charm is the essence, irreproducible, of the very flower of the language itself: hence the difficulty of representing, even partially, in any Western tongue, its subtler delicacies of sentiment, allusion, and color. But to understand the compositions of the people no scholarship is needed: they are characterized by the greatest possible simplicity, directness, and sincerity. The real art of them, in short, is their absolute artlessness. That was why I wanted them. Springing straight from the heart of the eternal youth of the race, these little gushes of song, like the untaught poetry of every people, utter what belongs to all human experience rather than to the limited life of a class or a time; and even in their melodies still resound the fresh and powerful pulsings of their primal source.

Manyemon had written down forty-seven songs; and with his help I made free renderings of the best. They were very brief, varying from seventeen to thirty-one syllables in length. Nearly all Japanese poetical metre consists of simple alternations of lines of five and seven syllables; the frequent exceptions which popular songs offer to this rule being merely irregularities such as the singer can smooth over either by slurring or by prolonging certain vowel sounds. Most of the songs which Manyemon had collected were of twenty-six syllables only; being composed of three successive lines of seven syllables each, followed by one of five, thus: —

> Ka-mi-yo ko-no-ka-ta
> Ka-wa-ra-nu mo-no wa:
> Mi-dzu no na-ga-ré to
> Ko-i no mi-chi.[1]

Among various deviations from this construction I found 7-7-7-7-5, and 5-7-7-7-5, and 7-5-7-5, and 5-7-5; but the classical five-line form (*tanka*), represented by 5-7-5-7-7, was entirely absent.

Terms indicating gender were likewise absent; even the expressions corresponding to "I" and "you" being seldom used, and the words signifying "beloved" applying equally to either sex. Only by the conventional value of some comparison, the use of a particular emotional tone, or the mention of some detail of costume, was the sex of the speaker suggested, as in this verse: —

I am the water-weed drifting, — finding no place of attachment:

Where, I wonder, and when, shall my flower begin to bloom?

[1] Literally, "*God-Age-since not-changed-things as-for: water-of flowing and love-of way.*"

Evidently the speaker is a girl who wishes for a lover: the same simile uttered by masculine lips would sound in Japanese ears much as would sound in English ears a man's comparison of himself to a violet or to a rose. For the like reason, one knows that in the following song the speaker is not a woman: —

> *Flowers in both my hands, — flowers of plum and cherry:*
> *Which will be, I wonder, the flower to give me fruit?*

Womanly charm is compared to the cherry flower and also to the plum flower; but the quality symbolized by the plum flower is moral always rather than physical.[1] The verse represents a man strongly attracted by two girls: one, perhaps a dancer, very fair to look upon; the other beautiful in character. Which shall he choose to be his companion for life?

One more example: —

> *Too long, with pen in hand, idling, fearing, and doubting,*
> *I cast my silver pin for the test of the tatamizan.*

Here we know from the mention of the hairpin that the speaker is a woman, and we can also suppose that she is a *geisha;* the sort of divination called *tatamizan* being especially

[1] See *Glimpses of Unfamiliar Japan,* ii. 357.

popular with dancing-girls. The rush covering of floor-mats (*tatami*), woven over a frame of thin strings, shows on its upper surface a regular series of lines about three fourths of an inch apart. The girl throws her pin upon a mat, and then counts the lines it touches. According to their number she deems herself lucky or unlucky. Sometimes a little pipe — geishas' pipes are usually of silver — is used instead of the hairpin.

The theme of all the songs was love, as indeed it is of the vast majority of the Japanese *chansons des rues et des bois;* even songs about celebrated places usually containing some amatory suggestion. I noticed that almost every simple phase of the emotion, from its earliest budding to its uttermost ripening, was represented in the collection; and I therefore tried to arrange the pieces according to the natural passional sequence. The result had some dramatic suggestiveness.

II

The songs really form three distinct groups, each corresponding to a particular period of that emotional experience which is the subject of all. In the first group of seven the surprise and pain and weakness of passion find utterance; beginning with a plaintive cry of reproach and closing with a whisper of trust.

I

You, by all others disliked! — oh, why must my heart thus like you?

II

This pain which I cannot speak of to any one in the world:
Tell me who has made it, — whose do you think the fault?

III

Will it be night forever? — I lose my way in this darkness:
Who goes by the path of Love must always go astray!

IV

Even the brightest lamp, even the light electric,
Cannot lighten at all the dusk of the Way of Love.

V

Always the more I love, the more it is hard to say so:
Oh! how happy I were should the loved one say it first!

VI

Such a little word! — only to say, "I love you"!
Why, oh, why do I find it hard to say like this?[1]

[1] Inimitably simple in the original: —

> Horeta wai na to
> Sukoshi no koto ga:
> Nazé ni kono yō ni
> Iinikui?

VII

Clicked-to [1] the locks of our hearts; let the keys remain in our bosoms.

After which mutual confidence the illusion naturally deepens; suffering yields to a joy that cannot disguise itself, and the keys of the heart are thrown away: this is the second stage.

I

*The person who said before, "I hate my life since I saw you,"
Now after union prays to live for a thousand years.*

II

*You and I together — lilies that grow in a valley:
This is our blossoming-time — but nobody knows the fact.*

III

*Receiving from his hand the cup of the wine of greeting,
Even before I drink, I feel that my face grows red.*

---

[1] In the original this is expressed by an onomatope, *pinto*, imitating the sound of the fastening of the lock of a *tansu*, or chest of drawers: —

> Pinto kokoro ni
> Jōmai oroshi:
> Kagi wa tagai no
>   Muné ni aru.

IV

I cannot hide in my heart the happy knowledge that fills it;
Asking each not to tell, I spread the news all round.[1]

V

All crows alike are black, everywhere under heaven.
The person that others like, why should not I like too?

VI

Going to see the beloved, a thousand ri are as one ri;[2]
Returning without having seen, one ri is a thousand ri.

VII

Going to see the beloved, even the water of rice-fields[3]
Ever becomes, as I drink, nectar of gods[4] *to the taste.*

---

[1] Much simpler in the original: —

>   Muné ni tsutsumenu
>   Uréshii koto wa; —
>   Kuchidomé shinagara
>   Furéaruku.

[2] One *ri* is equal to about two and a half English miles.

[3] In the original *dorota;* literally "mud rice-fields," — meaning rice-fields during the time of flushing, before the grain has fairly grown up. The whole verse reads: —

>   Horeté kayoyeba
>   Dorota no midzu mo
>   Noméba kanro no
>   Aji ga suru.

[4] *Kanro*, a Buddhist word, properly written with two Chinese characters signifying "sweet dew." The real meaning is *amrita*, the drink of the gods.

VIII

You, till a hundred years; I, until nine and ninety;
Together we still shall be in the time when the hair turns white.

IX

Seeing the face, at once the folly I wanted to utter
All melts out of my thought, and somehow the tears come first! [1]

X

Crying for joy made wet my sleeve that dries too quickly:
'T is not the same with the heart,—that cannot dry so soon!

XI

To Heaven with all my soul I prayed to prevent your going;
Already, to keep you with me, answers the blessed rain.

So passes the period of illusion. The rest is doubt and pain; only the love remains to challenge even death:—

I

Parted from you, my beloved, I go alone to the pine-field;
There is dew of night on the leaves; there is also dew of tears.

---

[1] Iitai guchi sayé
　Kao miriya kiyété
　　Tokaku namida ga
　　　Saki ni deru.

The use of *tokaku* ("somehow," for "some reason or other") gives a peculiar pathos to the utterance.

II

Even to see the birds flying freely above me
Only deepens my sorrow, — makes me thoughtful the more.

III

Coming ? or coming not ?   Far down the river gazing, —
Only yomogi shadows [1] *astir in the bed of the stream.*

IV

Letters come by the post; photographs give me the shadow !
Only one thing remains which I cannot hope to gain.

V

If I may not see the face, but only look at the letter,
Then it were better far only in dreams to see.

VI

Though his body were broken to pieces, though his bones on the
    shore were bleaching,
I would find my way to rejoin him, after gathering up the
    bones.[2]

---

[1] The plant *yomogi* (*Artemisia vulgaris*) grows wild in many of the half-dry beds of the Japanese rivers.

[2] Mi wa kuda kuda ni
   Honé wo isobé ni
   Sarasoto mama yo
   Hiroi atsumété
      Sōté misho.

The only song of this form in the collection. The use of the verb *soi* implies union as husband and wife.

III

Thus was it that these little songs, composed in different generations and in different parts of Japan by various persons, seemed to shape themselves for me into the ghost of a romance, — into the shadow of a story needing no name of time or place or person, because eternally the same, in all times and places.

Manyemon asks which of the songs I like best; and I turn over his manuscript again to see if I can make a choice. Without, in the bright spring air, the washers are working; and I hear the heavy *pon-pon* of the beating of wet robes, regular as the beating of a heart. Suddenly, as I muse, the voice of the boy soars up in one long, clear, shrill, splendid rocket-tone, — and breaks, — and softly trembles down in coruscations of fractional notes; singing the song that Manyemon remembers hearing when he himself was a boy: —

> *Things never changed since the Time of the Gods:*
> *The flowing of water, the Way of Love.*

"I think that is the best," I said. "It is the soul of all the rest."

"Hin no nusubito, koi no uta," interpretatively murmurs Manyemon. "Even as out of poverty comes the thief, so out of love the song!"

III

NOTES OF A TRIP TO KYŌTO

I

It had been intended to celebrate in spring the eleven hundredth anniversary of the foundation of Kyōto; but the outbreak of pestilence caused postponement of the festival to the autumn, and the celebration began on the 15th of the tenth month. Little festival medals of nickel, made to be pinned to the breast, like military decorations, were for sale at half a yen each. These medals entitled the wearers to special cheap fares on all the Japanese railroad and steamship lines, and to other desirable privileges, such as free entrance to wonderful palaces, gardens, and temples. On the 23d of October I found myself in possession of a medal, and journeying to Kyōto by the first morning train, which was overcrowded with people eager to witness the great historical processions announced for the

24th and 25th. Many had to travel standing, but the crowd was good-natured and merry. A number of my fellow-passengers were Ōsaka geisha going to the festival. They diverted themselves by singing songs and by playing ken with some male acquaintances, and their kittenish pranks and funny cries kept everybody amused. One had an extraordinary voice, with which she could twitter like a sparrow.

You can always tell by the voices of women conversing anywhere — in a hotel, for example — if there happen to be any geisha among them, because the peculiar timbre given by professional training is immediately recognizable. The wonderful character of that training, however, is fairly manifested only when the really professional tones of the voice are used, — falsetto tones, never touching, but often curiously sweet. Now, the street singers, the poor blind women who sing ballads with the natural voice only, use tones that draw tears. The voice is generally a powerful contralto; *and the deep tones are the tones that touch.* The falsetto tones of the geisha rise into a treble above the natural range of the adult voice, and as penetrating as a bird's. In a banquet-hall full of guests, you can distinctly hear, above all the sound of drums and samisen and chatter and laughter, the thin, sweet cry of the geisha playing ken, —

"*Futatsŭ! futatsŭ! futatsŭ!*" —

while you may be quite unable to hear the shouted response of the man she plays with, —

"*Mitsŭ! mitsŭ! mitsŭ!*"

II

The first surprise with which Kyōto greeted her visitors was the beauty of her festival decorations. Every street had been prepared for illumination. Before each house had been planted a new lantern-post of unpainted wood, from which a lantern bearing some appropriate design was suspended. There were also national flags and sprigs of pine above each entrance. But the lanterns made the charm of the display. In each section of street they were of the same form, and were fixed at exactly the same height, and were protected from possible bad weather by the same kind of covering. But in different streets the lanterns were different. In some of the wide thoroughfares they were very large; and while in some streets each was sheltered by a little wooden awning, in others every lantern had a Japanese paper umbrella spread and fastened above it.

There was no pageant on the morning of my arrival, and I spent a couple of hours delightfully at the festival exhibition of kakemono in the imperial summer palace called Omuro Gosho. Unlike the professional art display which I had seen in the spring, this represented chiefly the work of students; and I found it incomparably more original and attractive. Nearly all the pictures, thousands in number, were for sale, at prices ranging from three to fifty yen; and it was impossible not to buy to the limit of one's purse. There were studies of nature evidently made on the spot: such as a glimpse of hazy autumn rice-fields, with dragonflies darting over the drooping grain; maples crimsoning above a tremendous gorge; ranges of peaks steeped in morning mist; and a peasant's cottage perched on the verge of some dizzy mountain road. Also there were fine bits of realism, such as a cat seizing a mouse in the act of stealing the offerings placed in a Buddhist household shrine.

But I have no intention to try the reader's patience with a description of pictures. I mention my visit to the display only because of something I saw there more interesting than any picture. Near the main entrance was a specimen of handwriting, intended to be mounted as a kakemono later on, and temporarily fixed upon a board about three feet long by eighteen inches wide, — a Japanese poem. It was a wonder of calligraphy. Instead of the usual red stamp or seal with which the Japanese calligrapher marks his masterpieces, I saw the red imprint of a tiny, tiny hand, — a *living* hand, which had been smeared with crimson printing-ink and deftly pressed upon the paper. I could distinguish those little finger-marks of which Mr. Galton has taught us the characteristic importance.

That writing had been done in the presence of His Imperial Majesty by a child of six years, — or of five, according to our Western method of computing age from the date of birth. The prime minister, Marquis Ito, saw the miracle, and adopted the little boy, whose present name is therefore Ito Medzui.

Even Japanese observers could scarcely believe the testimony of their own eyes. Few adult calligraphers could surpass that writing. Certainly no Occidental artist, even after years of study, could repeat the feat performed by the brush of that child before the Emperor. Of course such a child can be born but once in a thousand years, — to realize, or almost realize, the ancient Chinese legends of divinely inspired writers.

Still, it was not the beauty of the thing in itself which impressed me, but the weird, extraordinary, indubitable proof it afforded of an inherited memory so vivid as to be almost equal to the recollection of former births. Generations of dead calligraphers revived in the fingers of that tiny hand. The thing was never the work of an individual child five years old, but beyond all question the work of ghosts, — the countless ghosts that make the compound ancestral soul. It was proof visible and tangible of psychological and physiological wonders justifying both the

Shintō doctrine of ancestor worship and the Buddhist doctrine of preëxistence.

III

After looking at all the pictures I visited the great palace garden, only recently opened to the public. It is called the Garden of the Cavern of the Genii. (At least "genii" is about the only word one can use to translate the term "Sennin," for which there is no real English equivalent; the Sennin, who are supposed to possess immortal life, and to haunt forests or caverns, being Japanese, or rather Chinese mythological transformations of the Indian Rishi.) The garden deserves its name. I felt as if I had indeed entered an enchanted place.

It is a landscape-garden, — a Buddhist creation, belonging to what is now simply a palace, but was once a monastery, built as a religious retreat for emperors and princes weary of earthly vanities. The first impression received after passing the gate is that of a grand old English park: the colossal trees, the shorn grass, the broad walks, the fresh sweet scent of verdure, all awaken English memories. But as you proceed farther these memories are slowly effaced, and the true Oriental impression defines : you perceive that the forms of those mighty trees are not European; various and surprising exotic details reveal themselves; and then you are gazing down upon a sheet of water containing high rocks and islets connected by bridges of the strangest shapes. Gradually, — only gradually, — the immense charm, the weird Buddhist charm of the place, grows and grows upon you; and the sense of its vast antiquity defines to touch that chord of the æsthetic feeling which brings the vibration of awe.

Considered as a human work alone, the garden is a marvel : only the skilled labor of thousands could have joined together the mere bones of it, the prodigious rocky skeleton of its plan. This once shaped and earthed and planted, Nature was left alone to finish the wonder. Working through ten centuries, she has surpassed — nay, unspeakably magnified — the dream of the artist. Without exact information, no stranger unfamiliar with the laws and the purpose of Japanese garden-construction could imagine that all this had a human designer some thousand years ago: the effect is that of a section of primeval forest, preserved untouched from the beginning, and walled away from the rest of the world in the heart of the old capital. The rock-faces, the great fantastic roots, the shadowed bypaths, the few ancient graven monoliths, are all cushioned with the moss of ages; and climbing things have developed stems a foot thick, that hang across spaces like monstrous serpents. Parts of the garden vividly recall some aspects of tropical nature in the Antilles; — though one misses the palms, the bewildering web and woof of lianas, the reptiles, and the sinister day-silence of a West Indian forest. The joyous storm of bird life overhead is an astonishment, and proclaims gratefully to the visitor that the wild creatures of this monastic paradise have never been harmed or frightened by man. As I arrived at last, with regret, at the gate of exit, I could not help feeling envious of its keeper: only to be a servant in such a garden were a privilege well worth praying for.

IV

Feeling hungry, I told my runner to take me to a restaurant, because the hotel was very far; and the kuruma bore me into an obscure street, and halted before a rickety-looking house with some misspelled English painted above the entrance. I remember only the word "forign." After taking off my shoes I climbed three flights of breakneck stairs, or rather ladders, to find in the third story a set of rooms furnished in foreign style. The windows were glass; the linen was satisfactory; the only things Japanese were the mattings and a welcome smoking-box. American chromo-lithographs decorated the walls. Nevertheless, I suspected that few foreigners had ever been in the house: it existed by sending out Western cooking, in little tin boxes, to native hotels; and the rooms had doubtless been fitted up for Japanese visitors.

I noticed that the plates, cups, and other utensils bore the monogram of a long-defunct English hotel which used to exist in one of the open ports. The dinner was served by nice-looking girls, who had certainly been trained by somebody accustomed to foreign service; but their innocent curiosity and extreme shyness convinced me that they had never waited upon a real foreigner before. Suddenly I observed on a table at the other end of the room something resembling a music-box, and covered with a piece of crochet-work! I went to it, and discovered the wreck of a herophone. There were plenty of perforated musical selections. I fixed the crank in place, and tried to extort the music of a German song, entitled "Five Hundred Thousand Devils." The herophone gurgled, moaned, roared for a moment, sobbed, roared again, and relapsed into silence. I tried a number of other selections, including "Les Cloches de Corneville;" but the noises produced were in all cases about the same. Evidently the thing had been bought, together with the monogram-bearing delft and britannia ware, at some auction sale in one of the foreign settlements. There was a queer melancholy in the experience, difficult to express. One must have lived in Japan to understand why the thing appeared so exiled, so pathetically out of place, so utterly misunderstood. Our harmonized Western music means simply so much noise to the average Japanese ear; and I felt quite sure that the internal condition of the herophone remained unknown to its Oriental proprietor.

An equally singular but more pleasant experience awaited me on the road back to the hotel. I halted at a second-hand furniture shop to look at some curiosities, and perceived, among a lot of old books, a big volume bearing in letters of much-tarnished gold the title, ATLANTIC MONTHLY. Looking closer, I saw "Vol. V. Boston: Ticknor & Fields. 1860." Volumes of The Atlantic of 1860 are not common anywhere. I asked the price; and the Japanese shopkeeper said fifty sen, because it was "a very large book." I was much too pleased to think of bargaining with him, and secured the prize. I looked through its stained pages for old friends, and found them, — all anonymous in 1865, many world-famous in 1895. There were installments of "Elsie Venner," under the title of "The Professor's Story;" chapters of "Roba di Roma;" a poem called "Pythagoras," but since renamed

"Metempsychosis," as lovers of Thomas Bailey Aldrich are doubtless aware; the personal narrative of a filibuster with Walker in Nicaragua; admirable papers upon the Maroons of Jamaica and the Maroons of Surinam; and, among other precious things, an essay on Japan, opening with the significant sentence, "The arrival in this country of an embassy from Japan, the first political delegation ever vouchsafed to a foreign nation by that reticent and jealous people, is now a topic of universal interest." A little farther on, some popular misapprehensions of the period were thus corrected: "Although now known to be entirely distinct, the Chinese and Japanese . . . were for a long time looked upon as kindred races, and esteemed alike. . . . We find that while, on close examination, the imagined attractions of China disappear, those of Japan become more definite." Any Japanese of this self-assertive twenty-eighth year of Meiji could scarcely find fault with The Atlantic's estimate of his country thirty-five years ago: "Its commanding position, its wealth, its commercial resources, and the quick intelligence of its people, — not at all inferior to that of the people of the West, although naturally restricted in its development, — give to Japan . . . an importance far above that of any other Eastern country." The only error of this generous estimate was an error centuries old, — the delusion of Japan's wealth. What made me feel a little ancient was to recognize in the quaint spellings Ziogoon, Tycoon, Sintoo, Kiusiu, Fide-yosi, Nobanunga, — spellings of the old Dutch and old Jesuit writers, — the modern and familiar Shōgun, Taikun, Shintō, Kyūshū, Hideyoshi, and Nobunaga.

I passed the evening wandering through the illuminated streets, and visited some of the numberless shows. I saw a young man writing Buddhist texts and drawing horses with his feet; the extraordinary fact about the work being that the texts were written backwards, — from the bottom of the column up, just as an ordinary calligrapher would write them from the top of the column down, — and the pictures of horses were always commenced with the tail. I saw a kind of amphitheatre, with an aquarium in lieu of arena, where mermaids swam and sang Japanese songs. I saw maidens "made by glamour out of flowers" by a Japanese cultivator of chrysanthemums. And between whiles I peeped into the toy-shops, full of novelties. What there especially struck me was the display of that astounding ingenuity by which Japanese inventors are able to reach, at a cost too small to name, precisely the same results as those exhibited in our expensive mechanical toys. A group of cocks and hens made of paper were set to pecking imaginary grain out of a basket by the pressure of a bamboo spring, — the whole thing costing half a cent. An artificial mouse ran about, doubling and scurrying, as if trying to slip under mats or into chinks: it cost only one cent, and was made with a bit of colored paper, a spool of baked clay, and a long thread; you had only to pull the thread, and the mouse began to run. Butterflies of paper, moved by an equally simple device, began to fly when thrown into the air. An artificial cuttlefish began to wriggle all its tentacles when you blew into a little rush tube fixed under its head.

When I decided to return, the lanterns were out, the shops were closing; and the streets darkened about me long before I reached the hotel. After the great glow of the illumination, the witchcrafts of the shows, the merry tumult, the sea-like sound of wooden sandals, this sudden coming of blankness and silence made me feel as if the previous experience had been unreal, — an illusion of light and color and noise made just to deceive, as in stories of goblin foxes. But the quick vanishing of all that composes a Japanese festival-night really lends a keener edge to the pleasure of remembrance: there is no slow fading out of the phantasmagoria, and its memory is thus kept free from the least tinge of melancholy.

V

While I was thinking about the fugitive charm of Japanese amusements, the question put itself, Are not all pleasures keen in proportion to their evanescence? Proof of the affirmative would lend strong support to the Buddhist theory of the nature of pleasure. We know that mental enjoyments are powerful in proportion to the complexity of the feelings and ideas composing them; and the most complex feelings would therefore seem to be of necessity the briefest. At all events, Japanese popular pleasures have the double peculiarity of being evanescent and complex, not merely because of their delicacy and their multiplicity of detail, but because this delicacy and multiplicity are adventitious, depending upon temporary conditions and combinations. Among such conditions are the seasons of flowering and of fading, hours of sunshine or full moon, a change of place, a shifting of light and shade. Among combinations are the fugitive holiday manifestations of the race genius: fragilities utilized to create illusion; dreams made visible; memories revived in symbols, images, ideographs, dashes of color, fragments of melody; countless minute appeals both to individual experience and to national sentiment. And the emotional result remains incommunicable to Western minds, because the myriad little details and suggestions producing it belong to a world incomprehensible without years of familiarity, — a world of traditions, beliefs, superstitions, feelings, ideas, about which foreigners, as a general rule, know nothing. Even by the few who do know that world, the nameless delicious sensation, the great vague wave of pleasure excited by the spectacle of Japanese enjoyment, can only be described as *the feeling of Japan*.

A sociological fact of interest is suggested by the amazing cheapness of these pleasures. The charm of Japanese life presents us with the extraordinary phenomenon of poverty as an influence in the development of æsthetic sentiment, or at least as a factor in deciding the direction and expansion of that development. But for poverty, the race could not have discovered, ages ago, the secret of making pleasure the commonest instead of the costliest of experiences, — the divine art of creating the beautiful out of nothing!

One explanation of this cheapness is the capacity of the people to find in everything natural — in landscapes, mists, clouds, sunsets, — in the sight of birds, insects, and flowers — a much keener pleasure than we, as the vividness of their artistic presentations of visual experience bears witness. Another explanation is that the national religions and the old-fashioned education have so developed imaginative power that it can be stirred into an activity of delight by anything, however trifling, able to suggest the traditions or the legends of the past.

Perhaps Japanese cheap pleasures might be broadly divided into those of time and place furnished by nature with the help of man, and those of time and place invented by man at the suggestion of nature. The former class can be found in every province, and yearly multiply. Some locality is chosen on hill or coast, by lake or river: gardens are made, trees planted, resting-houses built to command the finest points of view; and the wild site is presently transformed into a place of pilgrimage for pleasure-seekers. One spot is famed for cherry-trees, another for maples, another for wistaria; and each of the seasons — even snowy winter — helps to make the particular beauty of some resort. The sites of the most celebrated temples, or at least of the greater number of them, were thus selected, — always where the beauty of nature could inspire and aid the work of the religious architect, and where it still has power to make many a one wish that he could become a Buddhist or Shintō priest. Religion, indeed, is everywhere in Japan associated with famous scenery: with landscapes, cascades, peaks, rocks, islands; with the best places from which to view the blossoming of flowers, the reflection of the autumn moon on water, or the sparkling of fireflies on summer nights.

Decorations, illuminations, street displays of every sort, but especially those of holy days, compose a large part of the pleasures of city life which all can share. The appeals thus made to æsthetic fancy at festivals represent the labor, perhaps, of tens of thousands of hands and brains; but each individual contributor to the public effort works according to his particular thought and taste, even while obeying old rules, so that the total ultimate result is a wondrous, a bewildering, an incalculable variety. Anybody can contribute to such an occasion; and everybody does, for the cheapest material is used. Paper, straw, or stone makes no real difference: the art sense is superbly independent of the material. What shapes that material is perfect comprehension of something natural, something real. Whether a blossom made of chicken feathers, a clay turtle or duck or sparrow, a pasteboard cricket or mantis or frog, the idea is fully conceived and exactly realized. Spiders of mud seem to be spinning webs; butterflies of paper delude the eye. No models are needed to work from; — or rather, the model in every case is only the precise memory of the object or living fact. I asked at a doll-maker's for twenty tiny paper dolls, each with a different coiffure, — the whole set to represent the principal Kyōto styles of dressing women's hair. A girl went to work with white paper, paint, paste, thin slips of pine; and the dolls were finished in about the same time that an artist would have taken to draw a similar number of such figures. The actual time needed was only enough for the necessary digital movements, — not for correcting, comparing, improving: the image in the brain realized itself as fast as the slender hands could work. Thus most of the wonders of festival nights are created: toys thrown into existence with a twist of the fingers, old rags turned into figured draperies with a few motions of the brush, pictures made with sand. The same power of enchantment puts human grace under contribution. Children who on other occasions would attract no attention are converted into fairies by a few deft touches of paint and powder, and costumes devised for artificial light. Artistic sense of line and color suffices for any transformation. The tones of decoration are never of chance, but of knowledge: even the lantern illuminations prove this fact, certain tints only being used in combination. But the whole exhibition is as evanescent as it is wonderful. It vanishes much too quickly to be found fault with. It is a mirage that leaves you marveling and dreaming for a month after having seen it.

Perhaps one inexhaustible source of the contentment, the simple happiness, belonging to Japanese common life is to be found in this universal cheapness of pleasure. The delight of the eyes is for everybody. Not the seasons only nor the festivals furnish enjoyment: almost any quaint street, any truly Japanese interior, can give real pleasure to the poorest servant who works without wages. The beautiful, or the suggestion of the beautiful, is free as air. Besides, no man or woman can be too poor to own something pretty; no child need be without delightful toys. Conditions in the Occident are otherwise. In our great cities, beauty is for the rich; bare walls and foul pavements and smoky skies for our poor, and the tumult of hideous machinery, — a hell of eternal ugliness and joylessness invented by our civilization to punish the atrocious crime of being unfortunate, or weak, or stupid, or overconfident in the morality of one's fellow-man.

VI

When I went out, next morning, to view the great procession, the streets were packed so full of people that it seemed impossible for anybody to go anywhere. Nevertheless, all were moving, or rather circulating; there was a universal gliding and slipping, as of fish in a shoal. I find no difficulty in getting through the apparently solid press of heads and shoulders to the house of a friendly merchant, about half a mile away. How any crowd could be packed so closely, and yet move so freely, is a riddle to which Japanese character alone can furnish the key. I was not once rudely jostled. But Japanese crowds are not all alike: there are some through which an attempt to pass would be attended with unpleasant consequences. Of course the yielding fluidity of any concourse is in proportion to its gentleness; but the amount of that gentleness in Japan varies greatly according to locality. In the central and eastern provinces the kindliness of a crowd seems to be proportionate to its inexperience of "the new civilization." This vast gathering, of probably not less than a million persons, was astonishingly good-natured and good-humored, because the majority of those composing it were simple country folk. When the police finally made a lane for the procession, the multitude at once arranged itself in the least egotistical manner possible, — little children to the front, adults to the rear.

Though announced for nine o'clock, the procession did not appear till nearly eleven; and the long waiting in those densely packed streets must have been a strain even upon Buddhist patience. I was kindly given a kneeling-cushion in the front room of the merchant's house; but although the cushion was of the softest and the courtesy shown me of the sweetest, I became weary of the immobile posture at last, and went out into the crowd, where I could vary the experience of waiting by standing first on one foot, and then on the other. Before thus deserting my post, however, I had the privilege of seeing some very charming Kyōto ladies, including a princess, among the merchant's guests. Kyōto is famous for the beauty of its women; and the most charming Japanese woman I ever saw was in that house, — not the princess, but the shy young bride of the merchant's eldest son. That the proverb about beauty being only skin-deep "is but a skin-deep saying" Herbert Spencer has amply proved by the laws of physiology; and the same laws show that grace has a much more profound significance than beauty. The charm of the bride was just that rare form of grace which represents the economy of force in the whole framework of the physical structure, —

the grace that startles when first seen, and appears more and more wonderful every time it is again looked at. It is very seldom indeed that one sees in Japan a pretty woman who would look equally pretty in another than her own beautiful national attire. What we usually call grace in Japanese women is daintiness of form and manner rather than what a Greek would have termed grace. In this instance, one felt assured that long, light, slender, fine, faultlessly knit figure would ennoble any costume: there was just that suggestion of pliant elegance which the sight of a young bamboo gives when the wind is blowing.

To describe the procession in detail would needlessly tire the reader; and I shall venture only a few general remarks. The purpose of the pageant was to represent the various official and military styles of dress worn during the great periods of the history of Kyōto, from the time of its foundation in the eighth century to the present era of Meiji, and also the chief military personages of that history. At least two thousand persons marched in the procession, figuring daimyō, kugé, hatamoto, samurai, retainers, carriers, musicians, and dancers. The dancers were impersonated by geisha; and some were attired so as to look like butterflies with big gaudy wings. All the armor and the weapons, the ancient head-dresses and robes, were veritable relics of the past, lent for the occasion by old families, by professional curio-dealers, and by private collectors. The great captains — Oda Nobunaga, Kato Kiyomasa, Iyeyasu, Hideyoshi — were represented according to tradition; a really monkey-faced man having been found to play the part of the famous Taikō.

While these visions of dead centuries were passing by, the people kept perfectly silent, — which fact, strange as the statement may seem to Western readers, indicated extreme pleasure. It is not really in accordance with national sentiment to express applause by noisy demonstration, — by shouting and clapping of hands, for example. Even the military cheer is an importation; and the tendency to boisterous demonstrativeness in Tōkyō is probably as factitious as it is modern. I remember two impressive silences in Kobé during 1895.

The first was on the occasion of an imperial visit. There was a vast crowd; the foremost ranks knelt down as the Emperor passed; but there was not even a whisper. The second remarkable silence was on the return of the victorious troops from China, who marched under the triumphal arches erected to welcome them without hearing a syllable from the people. I asked why, and was answered, "We Japanese think we can better express our feelings by silence." I may here observe, also, that the sinister silence of the Japanese armies before some of the late engagements terrified the clamorous Chinese much more than the first opening of the batteries. Despite exceptions, it may be stated as a general truth that the deeper the emotion, whether of pleasure or of pain, and the more solemn or heroic the occasion, in Japan, the more naturally silent those who feel or act.

Some foreign spectators criticised the display as spiritless, and commented on the unheroic port of the great captains and the undisguised fatigue of their followers, oppressed under a scorching sun by the unaccustomed weight of armor. But to the Japanese all this only made the pageant seem more real; and I fully agreed with them. As a matter of fact, the greatest heroes of military history have appeared at their best in exceptional moments only; the stoutest veterans have known fatigue; and undoubtedly Nobunaga and Hideyoshi and Kato Kiyomasa must have more than once looked just as dusty, and ridden or marched just as wearily, as their representatives in the Kyōto procession. No merely theatrical idealism clouds, for any educated Japanese, the sense of the humanity of his country's greatest men: on the contrary, it is the historical evidence of that ordinary humanity that most endears them to the common heart, and makes by contrast more admirable and exemplary all of the inner life which was not ordinary.

After the procession I went to the Dai-Kioku-Den, the magnificent memorial Shintō temple built by the government, and described in a former book. On displaying my medal I was allowed to pay reverence to the spirit of good Kwammu-Tennō, and to drink a little rice wine in his honor, out of a new wine-cup of pure white clay presented by a lovely child-miko. After the libation, the little priestess packed the white cup into a neat wooden box and bade me take it home for a souvenir; one new cup being presented to every purchaser of a medal.

Such small gifts and memories make up much of the unique pleasure of Japanese travel. In almost any town or village you can buy for a souvenir some pretty or curious thing made only in that one place, and not to be found elsewhere. Again, in many parts of the interior a trifling generosity is certain to be acknowledged by a present, which, however cheap, will seldom fail to prove a surprise and a pleasure. Of all the things which I picked up here and there, in traveling about the country, the prettiest and the most beloved are queer little presents thus obtained.

VII

I wanted, before leaving Kyōto, to visit the tomb of Yuko Hatakeyama. After having vainly inquired of several persons where she was buried, it occurred to me to ask a Buddhist priest who had come to the hotel on some parochial business. He answered at once, "In the cemetery of Makkeiji." Makkeiji was a temple not mentioned in guide-books, and situated somewhere at the outskirts of the city. I took a kuruma forthwith, and found myself at the temple gate after about half an hour's run.

A priest, to whom I announced the purpose of my visit, conducted me to the cemetery, — a very large one, — and pointed out the grave. The sun of a cloudless autumn day flooded everything with light, and tinged with spectral gold the face of a monument on which I saw, in beautiful large characters very deeply cut, the girl's name, with the Buddhist prefix *Retsujo*, signifying chaste and true, —

RETSUJO HATAKEYAMA YUKO HAKA.

The grave was well kept, and the grass had been recently trimmed. A little wooden awning erected in front of the stone sheltered the offerings of flowers and sprays of shikimi, and a cup of fresh water. I did sincere reverence to the heroic and unselfish spirit, and pronounced the customary formula. Some other visitors, I noticed, saluted the spirit after the

Shintō manner. The tombstones were so thickly crowded about the spot that, in order to see the back of the monument, I found I should have to commit the rudeness of stepping on the grave. But I felt sure she would forgive me; so, treading reverently, I passed round, and copied the inscription: "*Yuko, of Nagasagori, Kamagawamachi . . . from day of birth always good. . . . Meiji, the twenty-fourth year, the fifth month, the twentieth day . . . cause of sorrow the country having . . . the Kyōto government-house to went . . . and her own throat cut . . . twenty and seven years . . . Tani Tetsuomi made . . . Kyōto-folk-by erected this stone is.*" The Buddhist Kaimyō read, "*Gi-yu-in-ton-shi-chu-myō-kyō,*" — apparently signifying, "Right-meaning and valiant woman, instantly attaining to the admirable doctrine of loyalty."

In the temple, the priest showed me the relics and mementos of the tragedy: a small Japanese razor, blood-crusted, with the once white soft paper thickly wrapped round its handle caked into one hard red mass; the cheap purse; the girdle and clothing, blood-stiffened (all except the kimono, washed by order of the police before having been given to the temple); letters and memoranda; photographs, which I secured, of Yuko and her tomb; also a photograph of the gathering in the cemetery, where the funeral rites were performed by Shintō priests. This fact interested me; for, although condoned by Buddhism, the suicide could not have been regarded in the same light by the two faiths. The clothing was coarse and cheap: the girl had pawned her best effects to cover the expenses of her journey and her burial. I bought a little book containing the story of her life and death, copies of her last letters, poems written about her by various persons, — some of very high rank, — and a clumsy portrait. In the photographs of Yuko and her relatives there was nothing remarkable: such types you can meet with every day and anywhere in Japan. The interest of the book was psychological only, as regarded both the author and the subject. The printed letters of Yuko revealed that strange state of Japanese exaltation in which the mind remains capable of giving all possible attention to the most trivial matters of fact, while the terrible purpose never slackens. The memoranda gave like witness: —

Meiji twenty-fourth year, fifth month, eighteenth day.
5 sen to kurumaya from Nihonbashi to Uyeno.
Nineteenth day.
5 sen to kurumaya to Asakusa Umamachi.
1 sen 5 rin for sharpening something to hair-dresser in Shitaya.
10 yen received from Sano, the pawnbroker in Baba.
20 sen for train to Shincho.
1 yen 2 sen for train from Hama to Shidzuoka.
Twentieth day.
2 yen 9 sen for train from Shidzuoka to Hama.
6 sen for postage-stamps for two letters.
14 sen in Kiyomidzu.
12 sen 5 rin for umbrella given to kurumaya.

But in strange contrast to the methodical faculty thus manifested was the poetry of a farewell letter, containing such thoughts as these: —

"The eighty-eighth night" [that is, from the festival of the Setsubun] "having passed like a dream, ice changed itself into clear drops, and snow gave place to rain. Then cherry-blossoms came to please everybody; but now, poor things! they begin to fall even before the wind touches them. Again a little while, and the wind will make them fly through the bright air in the pure spring weather. Yet it may be that the hearts of those who love me will not be bright, will feel no pleasant spring. The season of rains will come next, and there will be no joy in their hearts. . . . Oh! what shall I do? There has been no moment in which I have not thought of you. . . . But all ice, all snow, becomes at last free water; the incense buds of the kiku will open even in frost. I pray you, think later about these things. . . . Even now, for me, is the time of frost, the time of kiku buds: if only they can blossom, perhaps I shall please you much. Placed in this world of sorrow, but not to stay, is the destiny of all. I beseech you, think me not unfilial; say to none that you have lost me, that I have passed into the darkness. Rather wait and hope for the fortunate time that shall come."

The editor of the pamphlet betrayed rather too much of the Oriental manner of judging woman, even while showering generous praise upon one typical woman. In a letter to the authorities Yuko had spoken of a family claim, and this was criticised as a feminine weakness. She had, indeed, achieved the extinction of personal selfishness, but she had been "very foolish" to speak about her family. In some other ways the book was disappointing. Under the raw, strong light of its commonplace revelations, my little sketch, "Yuko," written in 1894, seemed for the moment much too romantic. And yet the real poetry of the event remained unlessened, — the pure ideal that impelled a girl to take her own life merely to give proof of the love and loyalty of a nation. No small, mean, dry facts could ever belittle that large fact.

The sacrifice had stirred the feelings of the nation much more than it had touched my own. Thousands of photographs of Yuko and thousands of copies of the little book about her were sold. Multitudes visited her tomb and made offerings there, and gazed with tender reverence at the relics in Makkeiji; and all this, I thought, for the best of reasons. If commonplace facts are repellent to what we are pleased, in the West, to call "refined feeling," it is proof that the refinement is factitious and the feeling shallow. To the Japanese, who recognize that the truth of beauty belongs to the inner being, commonplace details are precious: they help to accentuate and verify the conception of a heroism. Those poor blood-stained trifles — the coarse honest robes and girdle, the little cheap purse, the memoranda of a visit to the pawnbroker, the glimpses of plain, humble, every-day humanity shown by the letters and the photographs and the infinitesimal precision of police records — all serve, like so much ocular evidence, to perfect the generous comprehension of the feeling that made the fact. Had Yuko been the most beautiful person in Japan, and her people of the highest rank, the meaning of her sacrifice would have been far less intimately felt. In actual life, as a general rule, it is the common, not the uncommon person who does noble things; and the people, seeing best, by the aid of ordinary facts, what is heroic in one of their own class, feel themselves honored. Many of us in the West will have to learn our ethics over again from the common people. Our cultivated classes have lived so long in an atmosphere of false idealism, mere conventional humbug, that the real, warm, honest human emotions seem to them vulgar; and the natural and inevitable punishment is inability to see, to hear, to feel, and to think. There is more truth in the little verse poor Yuko wrote on the back of her mirror than in most of our conventional idealism: —

"*By one keeping the heart free from stain, virtue and right and wrong are seen clearly as forms in a mirror.*"

VIII

I returned by another way, through a quarter which I had never seen before, — all temples. A district of great spaces, — vast and beautiful and hushed as by enchantment. No dwellings or shops. Pale yellow walls only, sloping back from the roadway on both sides, like fortress walls, but coped with a coping or rooflet of blue tiles; and above these yellow sloping walls (pierced with elfish gates at long, long intervals), great soft hilly masses of foliage — cedar and pine and bamboo — with superbly curved roofs sweeping up through them. Each vista of those silent streets of temples, bathed in the gold of the autumn afternoon, gave me just such a thrill of pleasure as one feels on finding in some poem the perfect utterance of a thought one has tried for years in vain to express.

Yet what was the charm made with? The wonderful walls were but painted mud; the gates and the temples only frames of wood supporting tiles; the shubbery, the stonework, the lotos-ponds, mere landscape-gardening. Nothing solid, nothing enduring; but a combination so beautiful of lines and colors and shadows that no speech could paint it. Nay! even were those earthen walls turned into lemon-colored marble, and their tiling into amethyst; even were the material of the temples transformed into substance precious as that of the palace described in the Sutra of the Great King of Glory, — still the æsthetic suggestion, the dreamy repose, the mellow loveliness and softness of the scene, could not be in the least enhanced. Perhaps it is just because the material of such creation is so frail that its art is so marvelous. The most wonderful architecture, the most entrancing landscapes, are formed with substance the most imponderable, — the substance of clouds.

But those who think of beauty only in connection with costliness, with stability, with "firm reality," should never look for it in this land, — well called the Land of Sunrise, for sunrise is the hour of illusions. Nothing is more lovely than a Japanese village among the hills or by the coast when seen just after sunrise, — through the slowly lifting blue mists of a spring or autumn morning. But for the matter-of-fact observer, the enchantment passes with the vapors: in the raw, clear light he can find no palaces of amethyst, no sails of gold, but only flimsy sheds of wood and thatch and the unpainted queerness of wooden junks.

So perhaps it is with all that makes life beautiful in any land. To view men or nature with delight, we must see them through illusions, subjective or objective. How they appear to us depends upon the ethical conditions within us. Nevertheless, the real and the unreal are equally illusive in themselves. The vulgar and the rare, the seemingly transient and the seemingly enduring, are all alike mere ghostliness. Happiest he who, from birth to death, sees ever through some beautiful haze of the soul, — best of all, that haze of love which, like the radiance of this Orient day, turns common things to gold.

IV

DUST

"Let the Bodhisattva look upon all things as having the nature of space, — as permanently equal to space; without essence, without substantiality." — SADDHARMA-PUNDARÎKA.

I HAVE wandered to the verge of the town; and the street I followed has roughened into a country road, and begins to curve away through rice-fields toward a hamlet at the foot of the hills. Between town and rice-fields a vague unoccupied stretch of land makes a favorite playground for children. There are trees, and spaces of grass to roll on, and many butterflies, and plenty of little stones. I stop to look at the children.

By the roadside some are amusing themselves with wet clay, making tiny models of mountains and rivers and rice-fields; tiny mud villages, also, — imitations of peasants' huts, — and little mud temples, and mud gardens with ponds and humped bridges and imitations of stone-lanterns (*tōrō*); likewise miniature cemeteries, with bits of broken stone for monuments. And they play at funerals, — burying corpses of butterflies and *semi* (cicadæ), and pretending to repeat Buddhist sutras over the grave. To-morrow they will not dare to do this; for to-morrow will be the first day of the festival of the Dead. During that festival it is strictly forbidden to molest insects, especially semi, some of which have on their heads little red characters said to be names of Souls.

Children in all countries play at death. Before the sense of personal identity comes, death cannot be seriously considered; and childhood thinks in this regard more correctly, perhaps, than self-conscious maturity. Of course, if these little ones were told, some bright morning, that a playfellow had gone away forever, — gone away to be reborn elsewhere, — there would be a very real though vague sense of loss, and much wiping of eyes with many-colored sleeves; but presently the loss would be forgotten and the playing resumed. The idea of ceasing to exist could not possibly enter a child-mind: the butterflies and birds, the flowers, the foliage, the sweet summer itself, only play at dying; — they seem to go, but they all come back again after the snow is gone. The real sorrow and fear of death arise in us only through slow accumulation of experience with doubt and pain; and these little boys and girls, being Japanese and Buddhists, will never, in any event, feel about death just as you or I do. They will find reason to fear it for somebody else's sake, but not for their own, because they will learn that they have died millions of times already, and have forgotten the trouble of it, much as one forgets the pain of successive toothaches. In the strangely penetrant light of their creed, teaching the ghostliness of all substance, granite or gossamer, — just as those lately found X-rays make visible the ghostliness of flesh, — this their present world, with its bigger mountains and rivers and rice-fields, will not appear to them much more real than the mud landscapes which they made in childhood. And much more real it probably is not.

At which thought I am conscious of a sudden soft shock, a familiar shock, and know myself seized by the idea of Substance as Non-Reality.

This sense of the voidness of things comes only when the temperature of the air is so equably related to the temperature of life that I can forget having a body. Cold compels painful notions of solidity; cold sharpens the delusion of personality; cold quickens egotism; cold numbs thought, and shrivels up the little wings of dreams.

To-day is one of those warm, hushed days when it is possible to think of things as they are, — when ocean, peak, and plain seem no more real than the arching of blue emptiness above them. All is mirage, — my physical self, and the sunlit road, and the slow rippling of the grain under a sleepy wind, and the thatched roofs beyond the haze of the rice-fields, and the blue crumpling of the naked hills behind everything. I have the double sensation of being myself a ghost and of being haunted, — haunted by the prodigious luminous Spectre of the World.

There are men and women working in those

fields. Colored moving shadows they are; and the earth under them — out of which they rose, and back to which they will go — is equally shadow. Only the Forces behind the shadow, that make and unmake, are real, — therefore viewless.

Somewhat as Night devours all lesser shadow will this phantasmal earth swallow us at last, and itself thereafter vanish away. But the little shadows and the Shadow-Eater must as certainly reappear, — must rematerialize somewhere and somehow. This ground beneath me is old as the Milky Way. Call it what you please, — clay, soil, dust: its names are but symbols of human sensations having nothing in common with it. Really it is nameless and unnamable, being a mass of energies, tendencies, infinite possibilities; for it was made by the beating of that shoreless Sea of Birth and Death whose surges billow unseen out of eternal Night to burst in foam of stars. Lifeless it is not: it feeds upon life, and visible life grows out of it. Dust it is of Karma, waiting to enter into novel combinations, — dust of elder Being in that state between birth and birth which the Buddhist calls *Chū-U.*

It is made of forces, and of nothing else; and those forces are not of this planet only, but of vanished spheres innumerable.

Is there aught visible, tangible, measurable, that has never been mixed with sentiency? — atom that has never vibrated to pleasure or to pain? — air that has never been cry or speech? — drop that has never been a tear? Assuredly this dust has felt. It has been everything we know; also much that we cannot know. It has been nebula and star, planet and moon, times unspeakable. Deity also it has been, — the Sun-God of worlds that circled and worshiped in other æons. "*Remember, Man, thou art but dust!*" — a saying profound only as materialism, which stops short at surfaces. For what is dust? "Remember, Dust, thou hast been Sun, and Sun thou shalt become again! . . . Thou hast been Light, Life, Love; — and into all these, by ceaseless cosmic magic, thou shalt many times be turned again!"

For this Cosmic Apparition is more than evolution alternating with dissolution: it is infinite metempsychosis; it is perpetual palingenesis. Those old predictions of a bodily resurrection were not falsehoods; they were rather foreshadowings of a truth vaster than all myths and deeper than all religions.

Suns yield up their ghosts of flame; but out of their graves new suns rush into being. Corpses of worlds pass all to some solar funeral pyre; but out of their own ashes they are born again. This earth must die: her seas shall be Saharas. But those seas once existed in the sun; and their dead tides, revived by fire, will pour their thunder upon the coasts of another world. Transmigration — transmutation: these are not fables! What is impossible? Not the dreams of alchemists and poets; — dross may indeed be changed to gold, the jewel to the living eye, the flower into flesh. What is impossible? If seas can pass from world to sun, from sun to world again, what of the dust of dead selves, — dust of memory and thought? Resurrection there is, — but a resurrection more stupendous than any dreamed of by Western creeds. Dead emotions will revive as surely as dead suns and moons. Only, so far as we can just now discern, there will be no return of identical individualities. The reapparition will always be a recombination of the preëxisting, a readjustment of affinities, a reintegration of being informed with the experience of anterior being. The Cosmos is a Karma.

Merely by reason of illusion and folly do we shrink from the notion of self-instability. For what is our individuality? Most certainly it is not individuality at all: it is multiplicity incalculable. What is the human body? A form built up out of billions of living entities, an impermanent agglomeration of individuals called cells. And the human soul? A composite of quintillions of souls. We are, each and all, infinite compounds of fragments of anterior lives. And the universal process that continually dissolves and continually constructs personality has always been going on, and is even at this moment going on, in every one of us. What being ever had a totally new feeling, an absolutely new idea? All our emotions and thoughts and wishes, however changing and growing through the varying seasons of life, are only compositions and recompositions of the sensations and ideas and desires of other folk, mostly of dead people, — millions of billions of dead people. Cells and souls are themselves recombinations, present aggregations of past knittings of forces, — forces about which nothing is known save that they belong to the Shadow-Makers of universes.

Whether you (by *you* I mean any other agglomeration of souls) really wish for immortality as an agglomeration, I cannot tell. But I confess that "my mind to me a kingdom is" — not! Rather it is a fantastical republic, daily troubled by more revolutions than ever occurred in South America; and the nominal government, supposed to be rational, declares that an eternity of such anarchy is not desirable. I have souls wanting to soar in air, and souls wanting to swim in water (seawater, I think), and souls wanting to live in woods or on mountain tops. I have souls longing for the tumult of great cities, and souls longing to dwell in tropical solitude; — souls, also, in various stages of naked savagery; — souls demanding nomad freedom without tribute; — souls conservative, delicate, loyal to empire and to feudal tradition, and souls that are Nihilists, deserving Siberia; — sleepless souls, hating inaction, and hermit souls, dwelling in such meditative isolation that only at intervals of years can I feel them moving about; — souls that have faith in fetiches; — polytheistic souls; — souls proclaiming Islam; — and souls mediæval, loving cloister shadow and incense and glimmer of tapers and the awful altitude of Gothic glooms. Coöperation among all these is not to be thought of: always there is trouble, — revolt, confusion, civil war. The majority detest this state of things: multitudes would gladly emigrate. And the wiser minority feel that they need never hope for better conditions until after the total demolition of the existing social structure.

I an individual, — an individual soul! Nay, I am a population, — a population unthinkable for multitude, even by groups of a thousand millions! Generations of generations I am, æons of æons! Countless times the concourse now making me has been scattered, and mixed with other scatterings. Of what concern, then, the next disintegration? Perhaps, after trillions of ages of burning in different dynasties of suns, the very best of me may come together again.

If one could only imagine some explanation of the Why! The questions of the Whence and the Whither are much less troublesome, since the Present assures us, even though vaguely, of Future and Past. But the Why!

The cooing voice of a little girl dissolves my reverie. She is trying to teach a child brother how to make the Chinese character for Man, — I mean Man with a big M. First she draws in the dust a stroke sloping downwards from right to left, so: —

then she draws another curving downwards from left to right, thus: —

joining the two so as to form the perfect *ji*, or character, *hito*, meaning a person of either sex, or mankind: —

Then she tries to impress the idea of this shape on the baby memory by help of a practical illustration, — probably learned at school. She breaks a slip of wood in two pieces, and manages to balance the pieces against each other at about the same angle as that made by the two strokes of the character. "Now see," she says: "each stands only by help of the other. One by itself cannot stand. Therefore the *ji* is like mankind. Without help one person cannot live in this world; but by getting help and giving help everybody can live. If nobody helped anybody, all people would fall down and die."

This explanation is not philologically exact; the two strokes evolutionally standing for a pair of legs, — all that survives in the modern ideograph of the whole man figured in the primitive picture-writing. But the pretty moral fancy is much more important than the scientific fact. It is also one charming example of that old-fashioned method of teaching which invested every form and every incident with ethical signification. Besides, as a mere item of moral information, it contains the essence of all earthly religion, and the best part of all earthly philosophy. A world-priestess she is, this dear little maid, with her dove's voice and her innocent gospel of one letter! Verily in that gospel lies the only possible present answer to ultimate problems. Were its whole meaning universally felt, — were its whole suggestion of the spiritual and material law of love and help universally obeyed, — forthwith, according to the Idealists, this seemingly solid visible world would vanish away like smoke! For it has been written that in whatsoever time all human minds accord in thought and will with the mind of the Teacher, *there shall not remain even one particle of dust that does not enter into Buddhahood.*

V

ABOUT FACES IN JAPANESE ART

I

A VERY interesting essay upon the Japanese art collections in the National Library was read by Mr. Edward Strange at a meeting of the Japan Society held last year in London. Mr. Strange proved his appreciation of Japanese art by an exposition of its principles, — the subordination of detail to the expression of a sensation or idea, the subordination of the particular to the general. He spoke especially of the decorative element in Japanese art, and of the Ukiyo-yé school of color-printing. He remarked that even the heraldry of Japan, as illustrated in little books costing only a few pence each, contained " an education in the planning of conventional ornament." He referred to the immense industrial value of Japanese stencil designs. He tried to explain the nature of the advantage likely to be gained in the art of book illustration from the careful study of Japanese methods; and he indicated the influence of those methods in the work of such artists as Aubrey Beardsley, Edgar Wilson, Steinlen Ibels, Whistler, Grasset, Cheret, and Lantrec. Finally, he pointed out the harmony between certain Japanese principles and the doctrines of one of the modern Western schools of Impressionism.

Such an address could hardly fail to provoke adverse criticism in England, because it suggested a variety of new ideas. English opinion does not prohibit the importation of ideas: the public will even complain if fresh ideas be not regularly set before it. But its requirement of them is aggressive: it wants to have an intellectual battle over them. To persuade its unquestioning acceptance of new beliefs or thoughts, — to coax it to jump to a conclusion, — were about as easy as to make the mountains skip like rams. Though willing to be convinced, providing the idea does not appear "morally dangerous," it must first be assured of the absolute correctness of every step in the mental process by which the

ABOUT FACES IN JAPANESE ART 99

novel conclusion has been reached. That Mr. Strange's just but almost enthusiastic admiration of Japanese art could pass without challenge was not possible; yet one would scarcely have anticipated a challenge from the ranks of the Japan Society itself. The report, however, shows that Mr. Strange's views were received even by that society in the characteristic English way. The idea that English artists could learn anything important from the study of Japanese methods was practically pooh-poohed; and the criticisms made by various members indicated that the philosophic part of the paper had been either misunderstood or unnoticed. One gentleman innocently complained that he could not imagine " why Japanese art should be utterly wanting in facial expression." Another declared that there could never have been any lady like the ladies of the Japanese prints; and he described the faces therein portrayed as " absolutely insane."

Then came the most surprising incident of the evening, — the corroboration of these adverse criticisms by his excellency the Japanese Minister, with the apologetic remark that the prints referred to "were only regarded as common things in Japan." Common things! Common, perhaps, in the judgment of other generations; æsthetic luxuries to-day. The artists named were Hokusai, Toyokuni, Hiroshigé, Kuniyoshi, Kunisada! But his excellency seemed to think the subject trifling; for he took occasion to call away the attention of the meeting, irrelevantly as patriotically, to the triumphs of the war. In this he reflected faithfully the Japanese *Zeitgeist*, which can scarcely now endure the foreign praise of Japanese art. Unfortunately, those dominated by the just and natural martial pride of the hour do not reflect that while the development and maintenance of great armaments — unless effected with the greatest economical caution — might lead in short order to national bankruptcy, the future industrial prosperity of the country is likely to depend in no small degree upon the conservation and cultivation of the national art sense. Nay, those very means by which Japan won her late victories were largely purchased by the commercial results of that very art sense to which his excellency seemed to attach no importance. Japan must

ABOUT FACES IN JAPANESE ART 101

continue to depend upon her æsthetic faculty, even in so commonplace a field of industry as the manufacture of mattings; for in mere cheap production she will never be able to undersell China.

II

Although the criticisms provoked by Mr. Strange's essay were unjust to Japanese art, they were natural, and indicated nothing worse than ignorance of that art and miscomprehension of its purpose. It is not an art of which the meaning can be read at a glance: years of study are necessary for a right comprehension of it. I cannot pretend that I have mastered the knowledge of its moods and tenses, but I can say truthfully that the faces in the old picture-books and in the cheap prints of to-day, especially those of the illustrated Japanese newspapers, do not seem to me in the least unreal, much less "absolutely insane." There was a time when they did appear to me fantastic. Now I find them always interesting, occasionally beautiful. If I am told that no other European would say so, then I must declare all other

Europeans wrong. I feel sure that, if these faces seem to most Occidentals either absurd or soulless, it is only because most Occidentals do not understand them; and even if his excellency the Japanese Minister to England be willing to accept the statement that no Japanese women ever resembled the women of the Japanese picture-books and cheap prints, I must still refuse to do so.[1] Those pictures, I contend, are true, and reflect intelligence, grace, and beauty. I see the women of the Japanese picture-books in every Japanese street. I have beheld in actual life almost every normal type of face to be found in a Japanese picture-book: the child and the girl, the bride and the mother, the matron and the grandparent; poor and rich; charming or commonplace or vulgar. If I am told that

---

[1] That Japanese art is capable of great things in ideal facial expression is sufficiently proved by its Buddhist images. In ordinary prints the intentional conventionalism of the faces is hardly noticeable when the drawing is upon a small scale; and the suggestion of beauty is more readily perceived in such cases. But when the drawing has a certain dimension, — when the face-oval, for instance, has a diameter of more than an inch, — the same treatment may seem inexplicable to eyes accustomed to elaborated detail.

ABOUT FACES IN JAPANESE ART 103

trained art critics who have lived in Japan laugh at this assertion, I reply that they cannot have lived in Japan long enough, or felt her life intimately enough, or studied her art impartially enough, to qualify themselves to understand even the commonest Japanese drawing.

Before I came to Japan I used to be puzzled by the absence of facial expression in certain Japanese pictures. I confess that the faces, although not even then devoid of a certain weird charm, seemed to me impossible. Afterwards, during the first two years of Far-Eastern experience, — that period in which the stranger is apt to imagine that he is learning all about a people whom no Occidental can ever really understand, — I could recognize the grace and truth of certain forms, and feel something of the intense charm of color in Japanese prints; but I had no perception of the deeper meaning of that art. Even the full significance of its color I did not know: much that was simply true I then thought outlandish. While conscious of the charm of many things, the reason of the charm I could not guess. I imagined the apparent conventionalism of the faces to indicate the arrested development of an otherwise marvelous art faculty. It never occurred to me that they might be conventional only in the sense of symbols which, once interpreted, would reveal more than ordinary Western drawing can express. But this was because I still remained under old barbaric influences, — influences that blinded me to the meaning of Japanese drawing. And now, having at last learned a little, it is the Western art of illustration that appears to me conventional, undeveloped, semi-barbarous. The pictorial attractions of English weeklies and of American magazines now impress me as flat, coarse, and clumsy. My opinion on the subject, however, is limited to the ordinary class of Western illustration as compared with the ordinary class of Japanese prints.

Perhaps somebody will say that, even granting my assertion, the meaning of any true art should need no interpretation, and that the inferior character of Japanese work is proved by the admission that its meaning is not universally recognizable. Whoever makes such a criticism must imagine Western art to be everywhere equally intelligible. Some of it — the very best — probably is; and some of Japanese art also is. But I can assure the reader that the ordinary art of Western book illustration or magazine engraving is just as incomprehensible to Japanese as Japanese drawings are to Europeans who have never seen Japan. For a Japanese to understand our common engravings, he must have lived abroad. For an Occidental to perceive the truth, or the beauty, or the humor of Japanese drawings, he must know the life which those drawings reflect.

One of the critics at the meeting of the Japan Society found fault with the absence of facial expression in Japanese drawing as conventional. He compared Japanese art on this ground with the art of the old Egyptians, and held both inferior because restricted by convention. Yet surely the age which makes *Laocoön* a classic ought to recognize that Greek art itself was not free from conventions. It was an art which we can scarcely hope ever to equal; but it was more conventional than any existing form of art. And since it proved that even the divine could find development within the limits of artistic convention, the charge of formality is not a charge worth making against Japanese art. Somebody may respond that Greek conventions were conventions of beauty, while those of Japanese drawing have neither beauty nor meaning. But such a statement is possible only because Japanese art has not yet found its Winckelmann nor its Lessing, whereas Greek art, by the labor of generations of modern critics and teachers, has been made somewhat more comprehensible to us than it could have been to our barbarian forefathers. The Greek conventional face cannot be found in real life, no living head presenting so large a facial angle; but the Japanese conventional face can be seen everywhere, when once the real value of its symbol in art is properly understood. The face of Greek art represents an impossible perfection, a superhuman evolution. The seemingly inexpressive face drawn by the Japanese artists represents the living, the actual, the every-day. The former is a dream; the latter is a common fact.

III

A partial explanation of the apparent physiognomical conventionalism in Japanese drawing is just that law of the subordination of individualism to type, of personality to humanity, of detail to feeling, which the miscomprehended lecturer, Mr. Edward Strange, vainly tried to teach the Japan Society something about. The Japanese artist depicts an insect, for example, as no European artist can do: he makes it live; he shows its peculiar motion, its character, everything by which it is at once distinguished as a type, — and all this with a few brush-strokes. But he does not attempt to represent every vein upon each of its wings, every separate joint of its antennæ:[1] he depicts it as it is really seen at a glance, not as studied in detail. We never see all the details of the body of a grasshopper, a butterfly, or a bee, in the moment that we perceive it perching somewhere; we ob-

[1] Unless he carves it. In that case, his insect — cut in bone or horn or ivory, and appropriately colored — can sometimes scarcely be distinguished from a real insect, except by its weight, when held in the hand. Such absolute realism, however, is only curious, not artistic.

serve only enough to enable us to decide what kind of a creature it is. We see the typical, never the individual peculiarities. Therefore the Japanese artist paints the type alone. To reproduce every detail would be to subordinate the type character to the individual peculiarity. A very minute detail is rarely brought out except when the instant recognition of the type is aided by the recognition of the detail; as, for example, when a ray of light happens to fall upon the joint of a cricket's leg, or to reverberate from the mail of a dragonfly in a double-colored metallic flash. So likewise in painting a flower, the artist does not depict a particular, but a typical flower: he shows the morphological law of the species, or, to speak symbolically, nature's thought behind the form. The results of this method may astonish even scientific men. Alfred Russel Wallace speaks of a collection of Japanese sketches of plants as "the most masterly things" that he ever saw. "Every stem, twig, and leaf," he declares, "is *produced by single touches of the brush;* the character and perspective of very complicated plants being admirably given, and the articulations of stem and leaves shown in a most scientific manner." (The italics are my own.) Observe that while the work is simplicity itself, "produced by single touches of the brush," it is nevertheless, in the opinion of one of the greatest living naturalists, "most scientific." And why? Because it shows the type character and the law of the type. So again, in portraying rocks and cliffs, hills and plains, the Japanese artist gives us the general character, not the wearisome detail of masses; and yet the detail is admirably suggested by this perfect study of the larger law. Or look at his color studies of sunsets and sunrises: he never tries to present every minute fact within range of vision, but offers us only those great luminous tones and chromatic blendings which, after a thousand petty details have been forgotten, still linger in the memory, and there recreate the *feeling* of what has been seen.

Now this general law of the art applies to Japanese representations of the human figure, and also (though here other laws too come into play) of the human face. The general types are given, and often with a force that the cleverest French sketcher could scarcely emulate; the personal trait, the individual peculiarity, is not given. Even when, in the humor of caricature or in dramatic representation, facial expression is strongly marked, it is rendered by typical, not by individual characteristics, just as it was rendered upon the antique stage by the conventional masks of Greek actors.

IV

A few general remarks about the treatment of faces in ordinary Japanese drawing may help to the understanding of what that treatment teaches.

Youth is indicated by the absence of all but essential touches, and by the clean, smooth curves of the face and neck. Excepting the touches which suggest eyes, nose, and mouth, there are no lines. The curves speak sufficiently of fullness, smoothness, ripeness. For story-illustration it is not necessary to elaborate feature, as the age or condition is indicated by the style of the coiffure and the fashion of the dress. In female figures, the absence of eyebrows indicates the wife or

ABOUT FACES IN JAPANESE ART 111

widow; a straggling tress signifies grief; troubled thought is shown by an unmistakable pose or gesture. Hair, costume, and attitude are indeed enough to explain almost everything. But the Japanese artist knows how, by means of extremely delicate variations in the direction and position of the half dozen touches indicating feature, to give some hint of character, whether sympathetic or unsympathetic; and this hint is seldom lost upon a Japanese eye.[1] Again, an almost imperceptible hardening or softening of these touches has moral significance. Still, this is never

---

[1] In modern Japanese newspaper illustrations (I refer particularly to the admirable woodcuts illustrating the *feuilletons* of the Ōsaka *Asahi Shimbun*) these indications are quite visible even to a practiced foreign eye. The artist of the *Asahi Shimbun* is a woman.

I am here reminded of a curious fact which I do not remember having seen mention of in any book about Japan. The newly arrived Westerner often complains of his inability to distinguish one Japanese from another, and attributes this difficulty to the absence of strongly marked physiognomy in the race. He does not imagine that our more sharply accentuated Occidental physiognomy produces the very same effect upon the Japanese. Many and many a one has said to me, "For a long time I found it very hard to tell one foreigner from another: they all seemed to me alike."

individual: it is only the hint of a physiognomical law. In the case of immature youth (boy and girl faces), there is merely a general indication of softness and gentleness, — the abstract rather than the concrete charm of childhood.

In the portrayal of maturer types the lines are more numerous and more accentuated, — illustrating the fact that character necessarily becomes more marked in middle age, as the facial muscles begin to show. But there is only the suggestion of this change, not any study of individualism.

In the representation of old age, the Japanese artist gives us all the wrinkles, the hollows, the shrinking of tissues, the "crow's-feet," the gray hairs, the change in the line of the face following upon loss of teeth. His old men and women show character. They delight us by a certain worn sweetness of expression, a look of benevolent resignation; or they repel us by an aspect of hardened cunning, avarice, or envy. There are many types of old age; but they are types of human conditions, not of personality. The picture is not drawn from a model; it is not the reflection of an individual existence: its value is made by the recognition which it exhibits of a general physiognomical or biological law.

Here it is worth while to notice that the reserves of Japanese art in the matter of facial expression accord with the ethics of Oriental society. For ages the rule of conduct has been to mask all personal feeling as far as possible, — to hide pain and passion under an exterior semblance of smiling amiability or of impassive resignation. One key to the enigmas of Japanese art is Buddhism.

V

I have said that when I now look at a foreign illustrated newspaper or magazine I can find little pleasure in the engravings. Most often they repel me. The drawing seems to me coarse and hard, and the realism of the conception petty. Such work leaves nothing to the imagination, and usually betrays the effort which it cost. A common Japanese drawing leaves much to the imagination, — nay, irresistibly stimulates it, — and never betrays effort. Everything in a common European engraving is detailed and individualized. Everything in a Japanese drawing is impersonal and suggestive. The former reveals no law: it is a study of particularities. The latter invariably teaches something of law, and suppresses particularities except in their relation to law.

One may often hear Japanese say that Western art is too realistic; and the judgment contains truth. But the realism in it which offends Japanese taste, especially in the matter of facial expression, is not found fault with merely because of minuteness of detail. Detail in itself is not condemned by any art; and the highest art is that in which detail is most exquisitely elaborated. The art which saw the divine, which rose above nature's best, which discovered supramundane ideals for animal and even floral shapes, was characterized by the sharpest possible perfection of detail. And in the higher Japanese art, as in the Greek, the use of detail aids rather than opposes the aspirational aim. What most displeases in the realism of our modern illustration is not multiplicity of detail, but, as we shall presently see, *signification* of detail.

The queerest fact about the suppression of

physiognomical detail in Japanese art is that this suppression is most evident just where we should least expect to find it, namely, in those creations called "This-miserable-world pictures" (Ukiyo-yé), or, to use a corresponding Western term, "Pictures of this Vale of Tears." For although the artists of this school have really given us pictures of a very beautiful and happy world, they professed to reflect truth. One form of truth they certainly presented, but after a manner at variance with our common notions of realism. The Ukiyo-yé artist drew actualities, but not repellent or meaningless actualities; proving his rank even more by his refusal than by his choice of subjects. He looked for dominant laws of contrast and color, for the general character of nature's combinations, for the order of the beautiful as it was and is. Otherwise his art was in no sense aspirational; it was the art of the larger comprehension of things as they are. Thus he was rightly a realist, notwithstanding that his realism appears only in the study of constants, generalities, types. And as expressing the synthesis of common fact, the systematization of natural law, this Japanese art is by its method scientific in the true sense. The higher art, the aspirational art (whether Japanese or old Greek), is, on the contrary, essentially religious by its method.

Where the scientific and the aspirational extremes of art touch, one may expect to find some universal æsthetic truth recognized by both. They agree in their impersonality: they refuse to individualize. And the lesson of the very highest art that ever existed suggests the true reason for this common refusal.

What does the charm of an antique head express, whether in marble, gem, or mural painting, — for instance, that marvelous head of Leucothea which prefaces the work of Winckelmann? Needless to seek the reply from works of mere art critics. Science alone can furnish it. You will find it in Herbert Spencer's essay on Personal Beauty. The beauty of such a head signifies a superhumanly perfect development and balance of the intellectual faculties. All those variations of feature constituting what we call "expression" represent departures from a perfect type just in proportion as they represent what is termed "character;" — and they are, or ought to be, more or less disagreeable or painful because "the aspects which please us are the outward correlatives of inward perfections, and the aspects which displease us are the outward correlatives of inward imperfections." Mr. Spencer goes on to say that although there are often grand natures behind plain faces, and although fine countenances frequently hide small souls, "these anomalies do not destroy the general truth of the law any more than the perturbations of planets destroy the general ellipticity of their orbits."

Both Greek and Japanese art recognized the physiognomical truth which Mr. Spencer put into the simple formula, "*Expression is feature in the making.*" The highest art, Greek art, rising above the real to reach the divine, gives us the dream of feature perfected. Japanese realism, so much larger than our own as to be still misunderstood, gives us only "feature in the making," or rather, the general law of feature in the making.

VI

Thus we reach the common truth recognized equally by Greek art and by Japanese art, namely, the non-moral significance of individual expression. And our admiration of the art reflecting personality is, of course, non-moral, since the delineation of individual imperfection is not, in the ethical sense, a subject for admiration.

Although the facial aspects which really attract us may be considered the outward correlatives of inward perfections, or of approaches to perfections, we generally confess an interest in physiognomy which by no means speaks to us of inward *moral* perfections, but rather suggests perfections of the reverse order. This fact is manifested even in daily life. When we exclaim, "What force!" on seeing a head with prominent bushy brows, incisive nose, deep-set eyes, and a massive jaw, we are indeed expressing our recognition of force, but only of the sort of force underlying instincts of aggression and brutality. When we commend the character of certain strong aquiline faces, certain so-called Roman profiles, we are really commending the traits that mark a race of prey. It is true that we do not admire faces in which only brutal, or cruel, or cunning traits exist; but it is true also that we admire the indications of obstinacy, aggressiveness, and harshness when united with certain indications of intelligence. It may even be said that we associate the idea of manhood with the idea of aggressive power more than with the idea of any other power. Whether this power be physical or intellectual, we estimate it in our popular preferences, at least, above the really superior powers of the mind, and call intelligent cunning by the euphemism of "shrewdness." Probably the manifestation in some modern human being of the Greek ideal of masculine beauty would interest the average observer less than a face presenting an abnormal development of traits the reverse of noble, — since the intellectual significance of perfect beauty could be realized only by persons capable of appreciating the miracle of a perfect balance of the highest possible human faculties. In modern art we look for the feminine beauty which appeals to the feeling of sex, or for that child-beauty which appeals to the instincts of parenthood; and we should characterize real beauty in the portrayal of manhood not only as unnatural, but as effeminate. War and love are still the two dominant tones in that reflection of modern life which our serious art gives. But it will be noticed that when the artist would exhibit the ideal of beauty or of virtue, he is still obliged to borrow from antique knowledge. As a borrower, he is never quite successful, since he belongs to a humanity in many respects much below the ancient Greek level. A German philosopher has well said, "The resuscitated Greeks would, with perfect truth, declare our works of art in all departments to be thoroughly barbarous." How could they be otherwise in an age which openly admires intelligence less because of its power to create and preserve than because of its power to crush and destroy?

Why this admiration of capacities which we should certainly not like to have exercised against ourselves? Largely, no doubt, because we admire what we wish to possess, and we understand the immense value of aggressive power, intellectual especially, in the great competitive struggle of modern civilization.

As reflecting both the trivial actualities and the personal emotionalism of Western life, our art would be found ethically not only below Greek art, but even below Japanese. Greek art expressed the aspiration of a race toward the divinely beautiful and the divinely wise. Japanese art reflects the simple joy of existence, the perception of natural law in form and color, the perception of natural law in change, and the sense of life made harmonious by social order and by self-suppression. Modern Western art reflects the thirst of pleasure, the idea of life as a battle for the right to enjoy, and the unamiable qualities which are indispensable to success in the competitive struggle.

It has been said that the history of Western civilization is written in Western physiognomy. It is at least interesting to study Western facial expression through Oriental eyes. I have frequently amused myself by showing European or American illustrations to Japanese children, and hearing their artless comments upon the faces therein depicted. A complete record of these comments might prove to have value as well as interest; but for present purposes I shall offer only the results of two experiments.

The first was with a little boy, nine years old, before whom, one evening, I placed several numbers of an illustrated magazine. After turning over a few of the pages, he exclaimed, "Why do foreign artists like to draw horrible things?"

"What horrible things?" I inquired.

"These," he said, pointing to a group of figures representing voters at the polls.

"Why, those are not horrible," I answered. "We think those drawings very good."

"But the faces! There cannot really be such faces in the world."

"We think those are ordinary men. Really horrible faces we very seldom draw."

He stared in surprise, evidently suspecting that I was not in earnest.

To a little girl of eleven I showed some engravings representing famous European beauties.

"They do not look bad," was her comment. "But they seem so much like men, and their eyes are so big! . . . Their mouths are pretty."

The mouth signifies a great deal in Japanese physiognomy, and the child was in this regard appreciative. I then showed her some drawings from life, in a New York periodical. She asked, "Is it true that there are people like those pictures?"

"Plenty," I said. "Those are good, common faces, — mostly country folk, farmers."

"Farmers! They are like *Oni* [demons] from the *jigoku* [Buddhist hell]."

"No," I answered, "there is nothing very bad in those faces. We have faces in the West very much worse."

"Only to see them," she exclaimed, "I should die! I do not like this book."

I set before her a Japanese picture-book, — a book of views of the Tokaido. She clapped her hands joyfully, and pushed my half-inspected foreign magazine out of the way.

VI

NINGYŌ-NO-HAKA

MANYEMON had coaxed the child indoors, and made her eat. She appeared to be about eleven years old, intelligent, and pathetically docile. Her name was Iné, which means "springing rice;" and her frail slimness made the name seem appropriate.

When she began, under Manyemon's gentle persuasion, to tell her story, I anticipated something queer from the accompanying change in her voice. She spoke in a high thin sweet tone, perfectly even, — a tone changeless and unemotional as the chanting of the little kettle over its charcoal bed. Not unfrequently in Japan one may hear a girl or a woman utter something touching or cruel or terrible in just such a steady, level, penetrating tone, but never anything indifferent. It always means that feeling is being kept under control.

"There were six of us at home," said Iné, — "mother and father and father's mother, who was very old, and my brother and myself, and a little sister. Father was a *hyōguya*, a paper-hanger: he papered sliding-screens and also mounted kakemono. Mother was a hairdresser. My brother was apprenticed to a seal-cutter.

"Father and mother did well: mother made even more money than father. We had good clothes and good food; and we never had any real sorrow until father fell sick.

"It was the middle of the hot season. Father had always been healthy: we did not think that his sickness was dangerous, and he did not think so himself. But the very next day he died. We were very much surprised. Mother tried to hide her heart, and to wait upon her customers as before. But she was not very strong, and the pain of father's death came too quickly. Eight days after father's funeral mother also died. It was so sudden that everybody wondered. Then the neighbors told us that we must make a *ningyō-no-haka* at once,— or else there would be another death in our house. My brother said they were right; but he put off doing what they told him. Perhaps he did not have money enough, I do not know; but the haka was not made." . . .

"What is a *ningyō-no-haka?*" I interrupted.

"I think," Manyemon made answer, "that you have seen many *ningyō-no-haka* without knowing what they were; — they look just like graves of children. It is believed that when two of a family die in the same year, a third also must soon die. There is a saying, *Always three graves.* So when two out of one family have been buried in the same year, a third grave is made next to the graves of those two, and in it is put a coffin containing only a little figure of straw, — *wara-ningyō;* and over that grave a small tombstone is set up, bearing a kaimyō.[1] The priests of the temple to which the graveyard belongs write the kaimyō for these little gravestones. By making a *ningyō-no-haka* it is thought that a death may be prevented. . . . We listen for the rest, Iné."

---

[1] The posthumous Buddhist name of the person buried is chiseled upon the tomb or *haka.*

The child resumed: —

"There were still four of us, — grandmother, brother, myself, and my little sister. My brother was nineteen years old. He had finished his apprenticeship just before father died: we thought that was like the pity of the gods for us. He had become the head of the house. He was very skillful in his business, and had many friends: therefore he could maintain us. He made thirteen yen the first month; — that is very good for a seal-cutter. One evening he came home sick: he said that his head hurt him. Mother had then been dead forty-seven days. That evening he could not eat. Next morning he was not able to get up; — he had a very hot fever: we nursed him as well as we could, and sat up at night to watch by him; but he did not get better. On the morning of the third day of his sickness we became frightened — because he began to talk to mother. It was the forty-ninth day after mother's death, — the day the Soul leaves the house; — and brother spoke as if mother was calling him: — 'Yes, mother, yes! — in a little while I shall come!' Then he told us that mother was pulling him by the sleeve. He

would point with his hand and call to us: —
'There she is! — there! — do you not see
her?' We would tell him that we could not
see anything. Then he would say, 'Ah! you
did not look quick enough: she is hiding
now; — she has gone down under the floor-
mats.' All the morning he talked like that.
At last grandmother stood up, and stamped
her foot on the floor, and reproached mother,
— speaking very loud. 'Taka!' she said,
'Taka, what you do is very wrong. When you
were alive we all loved you. None of us ever
spoke unkind words to you. Why do you
now want to take the boy? You know that
he is the only pillar of our house. You know
that if you take him there will not be any one
to care for the ancestors. You know that if
you take him, you will destroy the family
name! O Taka, it is cruel! it is shameful!
it is wicked!' Grandmother was so angry that
all her body trembled. Then she sat down and
cried; and I and my little sister cried. But
our brother said that mother was still pulling
him by the sleeve. When the sun went down,
he died.

"Grandmother wept, and stroked us, and

sang a little song that she made herself. I can remember it still: —

> *Oya no nai ko to*
> *Hamabé no chidori:*
> *Higuré-higuré ni*
> *Sodé shiboru.*[1]

"So the third grave was made, — but it was not a *ningyō-no-haka;* — and that was the end of our house. We lived with kindred until winter, when grandmother died. She died in the night, — when, nobody knew: in the morning she seemed to be sleeping, but she was dead. Then I and my little sister were separated. My sister was adopted by a *tatamiya*, a mat-maker, — one of father's friends. She is kindly treated: she even goes to school!"

---

[1] "Children without parents, like the seagulls of the coast. Evening after evening the sleeves are wrung." The word *chidori* — indiscriminately applied to many kinds of birds, — is here used for seagull. The cries of the seagull are thought to express melancholy and desolation: hence the comparison. The long sleeve of the Japanese robe is used to wipe the eyes as well as to hide the face in moments of grief. To "wring the sleeve" — that is, to wring the moisture from a tear-drenched sleeve — is a frequent expression in Japanese poetry.

"*Aa fushigi na koto da! — aa komatta ne?*" murmured Manyemon. Then there was a moment or two of sympathetic silence. Iné prostrated herself in thanks, and rose to depart. As she slipped her feet under the thongs of her sandals, I moved toward the spot where she had been sitting, to ask the old man a question. She perceived my intention, and immediately made an indescribable sign to Manyemon, who responded by checking me just as I was going to sit down beside him.

"She wishes," he said, "that the master will honorably strike the matting first."

"But why?" I asked in surprise, — noticing only that under my unshod feet, the spot where the child had been kneeling felt comfortably warm.

Manyemon answered: —

"She believes that to sit down upon the place made warm by the body of another is to take into one's own life all the sorrow of that other person, — unless the place be stricken first."

Whereat I sat down without performing the rite; and we both laughed.

"Iné," said Manyemon, "the master takes

your sorrows upon him. He wants " — (I cannot venture to render Manyemon's honorifics) — " to understand the pain of other people. You need not fear for him, Iné."

VII

IN ŌSAKA

Takaki ya ni
Noborité miréba
Kemuri tatsu;—
Tami no kamado wa
Nigiwai ni kéri.

(When I ascend a high place and look about me, lo! the smoke is rising: the cooking ranges of the people are busy.)

Song of the Emperor NINTOKU.

I

NEARLY three hundred years ago, Captain John Saris, visiting Japan in the service of the "Right Honourable Companye, ye. marchants of London trading into ye. East Indyes," wrote concerning the great city of Ōsaka (as the name is now transliterated):—
"We found Osaca to be a very great towne, as great as London within the walls, with many faire timber bridges of a great height, seruing to passe ouer a riuer there as wide as the Thames at London. Some faire houses

we found there, but not many. It is one of the chiefe sea-ports of all Iapan; hauing a castle in it, maruellous large and strong" ... What Captain Saris said of the Ōsaka of the seventeenth century is almost equally true of the Ōsaka of to-day. It is still a very great city and one of the chief seaports of all Japan; it contains, according to the Occidental idea, "some faire houses;" it has many "faire timber bridges" (as well as bridges of steel and stone) — " seruing to passe ouer a river as wide as the Thames at London," — the Yodogawa; and the castle "marvellous large and strong," built by Hideyoshi after the plan of a Chinese fortress of the Han dynasty, still remains something for military engineers to wonder at, in spite of the disappearance of the many-storied towers, and the destruction (in 1868) of the magnificent palace.

Ōsaka is more than two thousand five hundred years old, and therefore one of the most ancient cities of Japan, — though its present name, a contraction of *Oye no Saka*, meaning the High Land of the Great River, is believed to date back only to the fifteenth century, before which time it was called Naniwa. Centuries before Europe knew of the existence of Japan, Ōsaka was the great financial and commercial centre of the empire; and it is that still. Through all the feudal era, the merchants of Ōsaka were the bankers and creditors of the Japanese princes: they exchanged the revenues of rice for silver and gold; — they kept in their miles of fireproof warehouses the national stores of cereals, of cotton, and of silk; — and they furnished to great captains the sinews of war. Hideyoshi made Ōsaka his military capital; — Iyeyasu, jealous and keen, feared the great city, and deemed it necessary to impoverish its capitalists because of their financial power.

The Ōsaka of 1896, covering a vast area has a population of about 670,000. As to extent and population, it is now only the second city of the empire; but it remains, as Count Okuma remarked in a recent speech, financially, industrially, and commercially superior to Tōkyō. Sakai, and Hyōgo, and Kōbé are really but its outer ports; and the last-named is visibly outgrowing Yokohama. It is confidently predicted, both by foreigners

IN OSAKA

and by Japanese, that Kobé will become the chief port of foreign trade, because Ōsaka is able to attract to herself the best business talent of the country. At present the foreign import and export trade of Ōsaka represents about $120,000,000 a year; and its inland and coasting trade are immense. Almost everything which everybody wants is made in Ōsaka; and there are few comfortable Japanese homes in any part of the empire to the furnishing of which Ōsaka industry has not contributed something. This was probably the case long before Tōkyō existed. There survives an ancient song of which the burden runs, — "*Every day to Ōsaka come a thousand ships.*" Junks only, in the time when the song was written; steamers also to-day, and deep-sea travelers of all rigs. Along the wharves you can ride for miles by a seemingly endless array of masts and funnels, — though the great Trans-Pacific liners and European mail-steamers draw too much water to enter the harbor, and receive their Ōsaka freight at Kobé. But the energetic city, which has its own steamship companies, now proposes to improve its port, at a cost of $16,000,000. An

Ōsaka with a population of two millions, and a foreign trade of at least $300,000,000 a year, is not a dream impossible to realize in the next half century. I need scarcely say that Ōsaka is the centre of the great trade-guilds,[1] and the headquarters of those cotton-spinning companies whose mills, kept running with a single shift twenty-three hours out of the twenty-four, turn out double the quantity of yarn per spindle that English mills turn out, and from thirty to forty per cent. more than the mills of Bombay.

Every great city in the world is believed to give a special character to its inhabitants; and in Japan the man of Ōsaka is said to be recognizable almost at sight. I think it can be said that the character of the man of the capital is less marked than that of the man of Ōsaka, — as in America the man of Chicago is more quickly recognized than the New Yorker or Bostonian. He has a certain quickness of perception, ready energy, and general air of being "well up to date," or even a little in advance of it, which represent the result

[1] There are upwards of four hundred commercial companies in Ōsaka.

IN OSAKA

of industrial and commercial intercompetition. At all events, the Ōsaka merchant or manufacturer has a much longer inheritance of business experience than his rival of the political capital. Perhaps this may partly account for the acknowledged superiority of Ōsaka commercial travelers; a modernized class, offering some remarkable types. While journeying by rail or steamer you may happen to make the casual acquaintance of a gentleman whose nationality you cannot safely decide even after some conversation. He is dressed with the most correct taste in the latest and best mode; he can talk to you equally well in French, German, or English; he is perfectly courteous, but able to adapt himself to the most diverse characters; he knows Europe; and he can give you extraordinary information about parts of the Far East which you have visited, and also about other parts of which you do not even know the names. As for Japan, he is familiar with the special products of every district, their comparative merits, their history. His face is pleasing, — nose straight or slightly aquiline, — mouth veiled by a heavy black moustache: the eyelids alone give you some right to suppose that you are conversing with an Oriental. Such is one type of the Ōsaka commercial traveler of 1896, — a being as far superior to the average Japanese petty official as a prince to a lackey. Should you meet the same man in his own city, you would probably find him in Japanese costume, — dressed as only a man of fine taste can learn how to dress, and looking rather like a Spaniard or Italian in disguise than a Japanese.

II

From the reputation of Ōsaka as a centre of production and distribution, one would imagine it the most modernized, the least characteristically Japanese, of all Japanese cities. But Ōsaka is the reverse. Fewer Western costumes are to be seen in Ōsaka than in any other large city of Japan. No crowds are more attractively robed, and no streets more picturesque, than those of the great mart.

Ōsaka is supposed to set many fashions; and the present ones show an agreeable tendency to variety of tint. When I first came to Japan the dominant colors of male costume were dark, — especially dark blue; any crowd of men usually presenting a mass of this shade. To-day the tones are lighter; and greys — warm greys, steel greys, bluish greys, purplish greys — seem to predominate. But there are also many pleasing variations, — bronze-colors, gold-browns, "tea-colors," for example. Women's costumes are of course more varied; but the character of the fashions for adults of either sex indicates no tendency to abandon the rules of severe good taste; — gay colors appearing only in the attire of children and of dancing-girls, — to whom are granted the privileges of perpetual youth. I may observe that the latest fashion in the silk upper-dress, or *haori*, of geisha, is a burning sky-blue, — a tropical color that makes the profession of the wearer distinguishable miles away. The higher-class geisha, however, affect sobriety in dress. I must also speak of the long overcoats or overcloaks worn out-of-doors in cold weather by both sexes. That of the men looks like an adaptation and modification of our "ulster," and has a little cape attached to it: the material is wool, and the color usually light brown or grey. That of the ladies, which has no cape, is usually of black broadcloth, with much silk binding, and a collar cut low in front. It is buttoned from throat to feet, and looks decidedly genteel, though left very wide and loose at the back to accommodate the bow of the great heavy silk girdle beneath.

Architecturally not less than fashionably, Ōsaka remains almost as Japanese as anybody could wish. Although some wide thoroughfares exist, most of the streets are very narrow, — even more narrow than those of Kyōto. There are streets of three-story houses and streets of two-story houses; but there are square miles of houses one story high. The great mass of the city is an agglomeration of low wooden buildings with tiled roofs. Nevertheless the streets are more interesting, brighter, quainter in their signs and signpainting, than the streets of Tōkyō; and the city as a whole is more picturesque than Tōkyō because of its waterways. It has not inaptly been termed the Venice of Japan; for it is traversed in all directions by canals, besides

IN OSAKA

being separated into several large portions by the branchings of the Yodogawa. The streets facing the river are, however, much less interesting than the narrow canals.

Anything more curious in the shape of a street vista than the view looking down one of these waterways can scarcely be found in Japan. Still as a mirror surface, the canal flows between high stone embankments supporting the houses, — houses of two or three stories, all sparred out from the stonework so that their façades bodily overhang the water. They are huddled together in a way suggesting pressure from behind; and this appearance of squeezing and crowding is strengthened by the absence of regularity in design, — no house being exactly like another, but all having an indefinable Far-Eastern queerness, — a sort of racial character, — that gives the sensation of the very-far-away in place and time. They push out funny little galleries with balustrades; barred, projecting, glassless windows with elfish balconies under them, and rooflets over them like eyebrows; tiers of tiled and tilted awnings; and great eaves which, in certain hours, throw shadows down to the foundation. As most of the timber-work is dark, — either with age or staining, — the shadows look deeper than they really are. Within them you catch glimpses of balcony pillars, bamboo ladders from gallery to gallery, polished angles of joinery, — all kinds of jutting things. At intervals you can see mattings hanging out, and curtains of split bamboo, and cotton hangings with big white ideographs upon them; and all this is faithfully repeated upside down in the water. The colors ought to delight an artist, — umbers and chocolates and chestnut-browns of old polished timber; warm yellows of mattings and bamboo screens; creamy tones of stuccoed surfaces; cool greys of tiling. . . . The last such vista I saw was bewitched by a spring haze. It was early morning. Two hundred yards from the bridge on which I stood, the house fronts began to turn blue; farther on, they were transparently vapory; and yet farther, they seemed to melt away suddenly into the light, — a procession of dreams. I watched the progress of a boat propelled by a peasant in straw hat and straw coat, — like the peasants of the old picture-books. Boat and man turned bright blue and then grey, and then, before my eyes, —— glided into Nirvana. The notion of immateriality so created by that luminous haze was supported by the absence of sound; for these canal-streets are as silent as the streets of shops are noisy.

No other city in Japan has so many bridges as Ōsaka: wards are named after them, and distances marked by them, — reckoning always from Koraibashi, the Bridge of the Koreans, as a centre. Ōsaka people find their way to any place most readily by remembering the name of the bridge nearest to it. But as there are one hundred and eighty-nine principal bridges, this method of reckoning can be of little service to a stranger. If a business man, he can find whatever he wants without learning the names of the bridges. Ōsaka is the best-ordered city, commercially, in the empire, and one of the best-ordered in the world. It has always been a city of guilds; and the various trades and industries are congregated still, according to ancient custom, in special districts or particular streets. Thus all the money-changers are

in Kitahama, — the Lombard Street of Japan;
the dry-goods trade monopolizes Honmachi;
the timber merchants are all in Nagabori and
Nishi-Yokobori; the toy-makers are in Mi-
nami Kiuhojimachi and Kita Midōmae; the
dealers in metal wares have Andojibashidōri
to themselves; the druggists are in Doshiō-
machi, and the cabinet-makers in Hachiman-
suji. So with many other trades; and so with
the places of amusement. The theatres are in
the Dōtombori; the jugglers, singers, dancers,
acrobats, and fortune-tellers in the Sennichi-
mae, close by.

The central part of Ōsaka contains many
very large buildings, — including theatres, re-
freshment-houses, and hotels having a reputation throughout the country. The number
of edifices in Western style is nevertheless
remarkably small. There are indeed between
eight and nine hundred factory chimneys; but
the factories, with few exceptions, are not constructed on Western plans. The really "foreign" buildings include a hotel, a prefectual
hall with a mansard roof, a city hall with a
classical porch of granite pillars, a good modern post-office, a mint, an arsenal, and sundry

IN OSAKA 145

mills and breweries. But these are so scattered and situated that they really make no particular impression at variance with the Far-Eastern character of the city. However, there is one purely foreign corner, — the old Concession, dating back to a time before Kobé existed. Its streets were well laid out, and its buildings solidly constructed; but for various reasons it has been abandoned to the missionaries, — only one of the old firms, with perhaps an agency or two, remaining open. This deserted settlement is an oasis of silence in the great commercial wilderness.[1] No attempts have been made by the native merchants to imitate its styles of building: indeed, no Japanese city shows less favor than Ōsaka to Occidental architecture. This is not through want of appreciation, but because of economical experience. Ōsaka will build in Western style — with stone, brick, and iron — only when and where the advantage of so

[1] The foreign legations left Ōsaka to take shelter at Kobé in 1868, during the civil war; for they could not be very well protected by their men-of-war in Ōsaka. Kobé once settled, the advantages offered by its deep harbor settled the fate of the Ōsaka Concession.

doing is indubitable. There will be no speculation in such constructions, as there has been at Tōkyō: Ōsaka "goes slow" and invests upon certainties. When there is a certainty, her merchants can make remarkable offers, — like that to the government two years ago of $56,000,000 for the purchase and reconstruction of a railway. Of all the houses in Ōsaka, the office of the "Asahi Shimbun" most surprised me. The "Asahi Shimbun" is the greatest of Japanese newspapers, — perhaps the greatest journal published in any Oriental language. It is an illustrated daily, conducted very much like a Paris newspaper, — publishing a *feuilleton*, translations from foreign fiction, and columns of light, witty chatter about current events. It pays big sums to popular writers, and spends largely for correspondence and telegraphic news. Its illustrations — now made by a woman — offer as full a reflection of all phases of Japanese life, old or new, as Punch gives of English life. It uses perfecting presses, charters special trains, and has a circulation reaching into most parts of the empire. So I certainly expected to find the "Asahi Shimbun" office

IN OSAKA

one of the handsomest buildings in Ōsaka. But it proved to be an old-time Samurai-yashiki,— about the most quiet and modest-looking place in the whole district where it was situated.

I must confess that all this sober and sensible conservatism delighted me. The competitive power of Japan must long depend upon her power to maintain the old simplicity of life.

III

Ōsaka is the great commercial school of the empire. From all parts of Japan lads are sent there to learn particular branches of industry or trade. There are hosts of applications for any vacancy; and the business men are said to be very cautious in choosing their *detchi*, or apprentice-clerks. Careful inquiries are made as to the personal character and family history of applicants. No money is paid by the parents or relatives of the apprentices. The term of service varies according to the nature of the trade or industry; but it is generally quite as long as the term of apprenticeship in Europe; and in some branches of business it may be from twelve to fourteen years. Such, I am told, is the time of service usually exacted in the dry goods business; and the detchi in a dry goods house may have to work fifteen hours a day, with not more than one holiday a month. During the whole of his apprenticeship he receives no wages whatever, — nothing but his board, lodging, and absolutely necessary clothing. His master is supposed to furnish him with two robes a year, and to keep him in sandals, or geta. Perhaps on some great holiday he may be presented with a small gift of pocket money; — but this is not in the bond. When his term of service ends, however, his master either gives him capital enough to begin trade for himself on a small scale, or finds some other way of assisting him substantially, — by credit, for instance. Many detchi marry their employers' daughters, in which event the young couple are almost sure of getting a good start in life.

The discipline of these long apprenticeships may be considered a severe test of character. Though a detchi is never addressed harshly, he has to bear what no European clerk would bear. He has no leisure, — no time of his own except the time necessary for sleep; he must work quietly but steadily from dawn till late in the evening; he must content himself with the simplest diet, must keep himself neat, and must never show ill-temper. Wild oats he is not supposed to have, and no chance is given him to sow them. Some detchi never even leave their shop, night or day, for months at a time, — sleeping on the same mats where they sit in business hours. The trained salesmen in the great silk stores are especially confined within doors, — and their unhealthy pallor is proverbial. Year after year they squat in the same place, for twelve or fifteen hours every day; and you wonder why their legs do not fall off, like those of Daruma.[1]

Occasionally there are moral break-downs. Perhaps a detchi misappropriates some of the shop money, and spends the same in riotous living. Perhaps he does even worse. But,

[1] In Japanese popular legend, Daruma (Bodhidharma), the great Buddhist patriarch and missionary, is said to have lost his legs during a meditation which lasted uninterruptedly for nine years. A common child's toy is a comical figure of Daruma, without legs, and so weighted within that, no matter how thrown down, it will always assume an upright position.

whatever the matter may be, he seldom thinks of running away. If he takes a spree, he hides himself after it for a day or two; — then returns of his own accord to confess, and ask pardon. He will be forgiven for two, three, perhaps even four escapades, — provided that he shows no signs of a really evil heart, — and be lectured about his weakness in its relation to his prospects, to the feelings of his family, to the honor of his ancestors, and to business requirements in general. The difficulties of his position are kindly considered, and he is never discharged for a small misdemeanor. A dismissal would probably ruin him for life; and every care is taken to open his eyes to certain dangers. Ōsaka is really the most unsafe place in Japan to play the fool in; — its dangerous and vicious classes are more to be feared than those of the capital; and the daily news of the great city furnishes the apprentice with terrible examples of men reduced to poverty or driven to self-destruction through neglect of those very rules of conduct which it is part of his duty to learn.

In cases where detchi are taken into service

at a very early age, and brought up in the shop almost like adopted sons, a very strong bond of affection between master and apprentice is sometimes established. Instances of extraordinary devotion to masters, or members of masters' households, are often reported. Sometimes the bankrupt merchant is reëstablished in business by his former clerk. Sometimes, again, the affection of a detchi may exhibit itself in strange extremes. Last year there was a curious case. The only son of a merchant — a lad of twelve — died of cholera during the epidemic. A detchi of fourteen, who had been much attached to the dead boy, committed suicide shortly after the funeral by throwing himself down in front of a train. He left a letter, of which the following is a tolerably close translation, — the selfish pronouns being absent in the original:

"Very long time in, august help received; — honorable mercy even, not in words to be declared. Now going to die, unfaithful in excess; — yet another state in, making rebirth, honorable mercy will repay. Spirit anxious only in the matter of little sister

O-Noto;— with humble salutation, that she be honorably seen to, supplicate.

"*To the August Lord Master,*
"*From*
"*MANO YOSHIMATSU.*"

IV

It is not true that Old Japan is rapidly disappearing. It cannot disappear within at least another hundred years; perhaps it will never entirely disappear. Many curious and beautiful things have vanished; but Old Japan survives in art, in faith, in customs and habits, in the hearts and the homes of the people: it may be found everywhere by those who know how to look for it, — and nowhere more easily than in this great city of ship-building, watch-making, beer-brewing, and cotton-spinning. I confess that I went to Ōsaka chiefly to see the temples, especially the famous Tennōji.

Tennōji, or, more correctly, Shitennōji, the Temple of the Four Deva Kings,[1] is one of

---

[1] They defend the four quarters of the world. In Japanese their names are Jikoku, Komoku, Zocho, Bishamon (or Tamon); — in Sanscrit, Dhritarashtra, Virupaksha, Virudhaka, and Vaisravana, — the Kuvera of Brahmanism.

the oldest Buddhist temples in Japan. It was founded early in the seventh century by Umayado-no-Oji, now called Shōtoku Taishi, son of the Emperor Yōmei, and prince regent under the Empress Suiko (572–621 A. D.). He has been well called the Constantine of Japanese Buddhism; for he decided the future of Buddhism in the Empire, first by a great battle in the reign of his father, Yomei Tennō, and afterwards by legal enactments and by the patronage of Buddhist learning. The previous Emperor, Bitatsu Tennō, had permitted the preaching of Buddhism by Korean priests, and had built two temples. But under the reign of Yomei, one Mononobé no Moriya, a powerful noble, and a bitter opponent of the foreign religion, rebelled against such tolerance, burned the temples, banished the priests, and offered battle to the imperial forces. These, tradition says, were being driven back when the Emperor's son — then only sixteen years old — vowed if victorious to build a temple to the Four Deva Kings. Instantly at his side in the fight there towered a colossal figure from before whose face the powers of Moriya broke and fled away. The rout of the enemies of Buddhism was complete and terrible; and the young prince, thereafter called Shōtoku Taishi, kept his vow. The temple of Tennōji was built, and the wealth of the rebel Moriya applied to its maintenance. In that part of it called the Kondō, or Hall of Gold, Shōtoku Taishi enshrined the first Buddhist image ever brought to Japan, — a figure of Nyo-i-rin Kwannon, or Kwannon of the Circle of Wishes, — and the statue is still shown to the public on certain festival days. The tremendous apparition in the battle is said to have been one of the Four Kings, — Bishamon (Vaisravana), worshiped to this day as a giver of victory.

The sensation received on passing out of the bright, narrow, busy streets of shops into the mouldering courts of Tennōji is indescribable. Even for a Japanese I imagine it must be like a sensation of the supernatural, — a return in memory to the life of twelve hundred years ago, to the time of the earliest Buddhist mission work in Japan. Symbols of the faith, that elsewhere had become for me conventionally familiar, here seemed but half familiar, exotic, prototypal; and things never before seen gave me the startling notion of a time and place out of existing life. As a matter of fact, very little remains of the original structure of the temple; parts have been burned, parts renovated. But the impression is still very peculiar, because the rebuilders and the renovators always followed the original plans, made by some great Korean or Chinese architect. Any attempt to write of the antique aspect, the queer melancholy beauty of the place, would be hopeless. To know what Tennōji is, one must see the weirdness of its decay, — the beautiful neutral tones of old timbers, the fading spectral greys and yellows of wall-surfaces, the eccentricities of disjointing, the extraordinary carvings under eaves, — carvings of waves and clouds and dragons and demons, once splendid with lacquer and gold, now time-whitened to the tint of smoke, and looking as if about to curl away like smoke and vanish. The most remarkable of these carvings belong to a fantastic five-storied pagoda, now ruinous: nearly all the brazen wind-bells suspended to the angles of its tiers of roofs have fallen. Pagoda and temple proper occupy a quadrangular court surrounded by an open cloister. Beyond are other courts, a Buddhist school, and an immense pond peopled by tortoises and crossed by a massive stone bridge. There are statues and stone lamps and lions and an enormous temple-drum; — there are booths for the sale of toys and oddities; — there are resting-places where tea is served, and cake-stands where you can buy cakes for the tortoises or for a pet deer, which approaches the visitor, bowing its sleek head to beg. There is a two-storied gateway guarded by huge images of the Ni-Ō, — Ni-Ō with arms and legs muscled like the limbs of kings in the Assyrian sculptures, and bodies speckled all over with little balls of white paper spat upon them by the faithful. There is another gateway whose chambers are empty; — perhaps they once contained images of the Four Deva Kings. There are ever so many curious things; but I shall only venture to describe two or three of my queerest experiences.

First of all, I found the confirmation of a certain suspicion that had come to me as I entered the temple precincts, — the suspicion that the forms of worship were peculiar as the

IN OSAKA   157

buildings. I can give no reason for this feeling; I can only say that, immediately after passing the outer gate, I had a premonition of being about to see the extraordinary in religion as well as in architecture. And I presently saw it in the bell-tower, — a two-story Chinese-looking structure, where there is a bell called the Indō-no-Kané, or Guiding-Bell, because its sounds guide the ghosts of children through the dark. The lower chamber of the bell-tower is fitted up as a chapel. At the first glance I noticed only that a Buddhist service was going on; I saw tapers burning, the golden glimmer of a shrine, incense smoking, a priest at prayer, women and children kneeling. But as I stopped for a moment before the entrance to observe the image in the shrine, I suddenly became aware of the unfamiliar, the astonishing. On shelves and stands at either side of the shrine, and above it and below it and beyond it, were ranged hundreds of children's ihai, or mortuary tablets, and with them thousands of toys; little dogs and horses and cows, and warriors and drums and trumpets, and pasteboard armor and wooden swords, and dolls and kites and masks and monkeys, and models of boats, and baby tea-sets and baby-furniture, and whirligigs and comical images of the Gods of Good Fortune, — toys modern and toys of fashion forgotten, — toys accumulated through centuries, — toys of whole generations of dead children. From the ceiling, and close to the entrance, hung down a great heavy bell-rope, nearly four inches in diameter and of many colors, — the rope of the Indō-Kané. *And that rope was made of the bibs of dead children,* — yellow, blue, scarlet, purple bibs, and bibs of all intermediate shades. The ceiling itself was invisible, — hidden from view by hundreds of tiny dresses suspended, — dresses of dead children. Little boys and girls, kneeling or playing on the matting beside the priest, had brought toys with them, to be deposited in the chapel, before the tablet of some lost brother or sister. Every moment some bereaved father or mother would come to the door, pull the bell-rope, throw some copper money on the matting, and make a prayer. Each time the bell sounds, some little ghost is believed to hear, — perhaps even to find its way back for one more look at loved toys and faces. The plaintive murmur of *Namu Amida Butsu;* the clanging of the bell; the deep humming of the priest's voice, reciting the Sutras; the tinkle of falling coin; the sweet, heavy smell of incense; the passionless golden beauty of the Buddha in his shrine; the colorific radiance of the toys; the shadowing of the baby-dresses; the variegated wonder of that bell-rope of bibs; the happy laughter of the little folk at play on the floor, — all made for me an experience of weird pathos never to be forgotten.

Not far from the bell-tower is another curious building, which shelters a sacred spring. In the middle of the floor is an opening, perhaps ten feet long by eight wide, surrounded by a railing. Looking down over the railing, you see, in the dimness below, a large stone basin, into which water is pouring from the mouth of a great stone tortoise, black with age, and only half visible, — its hinder part reaching back into the darkness under the floor. This water is called the Spring of the Tortoise, — Kamé-i-Sui. The basin into which it flows is more than half full of white paper, — countless slips of white paper, each bearing in Chinese text the kaimyō, or Buddhist posthumous name of a dead person. In a matted recess of the building sits a priest who for a small fee writes the kaimyō. The purchaser — relative or friend of the dead — puts one end of the written slip into the mouth of a bamboo cup, or rather bamboo joint, fixed at right angles to the end of a long pole. By aid of this pole he lowers the paper, with the written side up, to the mouth of the tortoise, and holds it under the gush of water, — repeating a Buddhist invocation the while, — till it is washed out into the basin. When I visited the spring there was a dense crowd; and several kaimyō were being held under the mouth of the tortoise; — numbers of pious folk meantime waiting, with papers in their hands, for a chance to use the poles. The murmuring of *Namu Amida Butsu* was itself like the sound of rushing water. I was told that the basin becomes filled with kaimyō every few days; — then it is emptied, and the papers burned. If this be true, it is a remarkable proof of the force of Buddhist faith in this busy commercial city;

for many thousands of such slips of paper would be needed to fill the basin. It is said that the water bears the names of the dead and the prayers of the living to Shōtoku Taishi, who uses his powers of intercession with Amida on behalf of the faithful.

In the chapel called the Taishi-Dō there are statues of Shōtoku Taishi and his attendants. The figure of the prince, seated upon a chair of honor, is life-size and colored; he is attired in the fashion of twelve hundred years ago, wearing a picturesque cap, and Chinese or Korean shoes with points turned up. One may see the same costume in the designs upon very old porcelains or very old screens. But the face, in spite of its drooping Chinese moustaches, is a typical Japanese face, — dignified, kindly, passionless. I turned from the faces of the statues to the faces of the people about me to see the same types, — to meet the same quiet, half-curious, inscrutable gaze.

In powerful contrast to the ancient structures of Tennōji are the vast Nishi and Higashi Hongwanji, almost exact counterparts of the

Nishi and Higashi Hongwanji of Tōkyō. Nearly every great city of Japan has a pair of such Hongwanji (Temples of the True Vow) — one belonging to the Western (Nishi), the other to the Eastern (Higashi) branch of this great Shin sect, founded in the thirteenth century.[1] Varying in dimension according to the wealth and religious importance of the locality, but usually built upon the same general plan, they may be said to represent the most modern and the most purely Japanese form of Buddhist architecture, — immense, dignified, magnificent.

But they likewise represent the almost protestant severity of the rite in regard to symbols, icons, and external forms. Their plain and ponderous gates are never guarded by the giant Ni-Ō; — there is no swarming of dragons and demons under their enormous eaves;

---

[1] The division of the sect during the seventeenth century into two branches had a political, not a religious cause; and the sections remain religiously united. Their abbots are of Imperial descent, whence their title of Monzeki, or Imperial Offspring. Travelers may observe that the walls inclosing the temple grounds of this sect bear the same decorative mouldings as those of the walls of the Imperial residences.

— no golden hosts of Buddhas or Bodhisattvas rise, rank on rank, by tiers of aureoles, through the twilight of their sanctuaries; — no curious or touching witnesses of grateful faith are ever suspended from their high ceilings, or hung before their altars, or fastened to the gratings of their doorways; — they contain no ex-votos, no paper knots recording prayer, no symbolic image but one, — and that usually small, — the figure of Amida. Probably the reader knows that the Hongwanji sect represents a movement in Buddhism not altogether unlike that which Unitarianism represents in Liberal Christianity. In its rejection of celibacy and of all ascetic practices; its prohibition of charms, divinations, votive offerings, and even of all prayer excepting prayer for salvation; its insistence upon industrious effort as the duty of life; its maintenance of the sanctity of marriage as a religious bond; its doctrine of one eternal Buddha as Father and Saviour; its promise of Paradise after death as the immediate reward of a good life; and, above all, in its educational zeal, — the religion of the "Sect of the Pure Land" may be justly said to have much in common with the progressive forms of Western Christianity, and it has certainly won the respect of the few men of culture who find their way into the missionary legion. Judged by its wealth, its respectability, and its antagonism to the grosser forms of Buddhist superstition, it might be supposed the least emotional of all forms of Buddhism. But in some respects it is probably the most emotional. No other Buddhist sect can make such appeals to the faith and love of the common people as those which brought into being the amazing Eastern Hongwanji temple of Kyōto. Yet while able to reach the simplest minds by special methods of doctrinal teaching, the Hongwanji cult can make equally strong appeal to the intellectual classes by reason of its scholarship. Not a few of its priests are graduates of the leading universities of the West; and some have won European reputations in various departments of Buddhist learning. Whether the older Buddhist sects are likely to dwindle away before the constantly increasing power of the Shinshū is at least an interesting question. Certainly the latter has everything in its favor,

— imperial recognition, wealth, culture, and solidity of organization. On the other hand, one is tempted to doubt the efficacy of such advantages in a warfare against habits of thought and feeling older by many centuries than Shinshū. Perhaps the Occident furnishes a precedent on which to base predictions. Remembering how strong Roman Catholicism remains to-day, how little it has changed since the days of Luther, how impotent our progressive creeds to satisfy the old spiritual hunger for some visible object of worship, — something to touch, or put close to the heart, — it becomes difficult to believe that the iconolatry of the more ancient Buddhist sects will not continue for hundreds of years to keep a large place in popular affection. Again, it is worthy of remark that one curious obstacle to the expansion of the Shinshū is to be found in a very deeply rooted race feeling on the subject of self-sacrifice. Although much corruption undoubtedly exists in the older sects, — although numbers of their priests do not even pretend to observe the vows regarding diet and celibacy,[1] — the

[1] This has been especially the case since the abrogation

ancient ideals are by no means dead; and the majority of Japanese Buddhists still disapprove of the relatively pleasurable lives of the Shinshū priesthood. In some of the remoter provinces, where Shinshū is viewed with especial disfavor, one may often hear children singing a naughty song (*Shinshū bozu e mon da!*), which might thus be freely rendered: —

> Shinshū priest to be, —
> What a nice thing!
> Wife has, child has,
> Good fish eats.

It reminded me of those popular criticisms of Buddhist conduct uttered in the time of the Buddha himself, and so often recorded in the Vinaya texts, — almost like a refrain: — "*Then the people were annoyed; and they murmured and complained, saying: 'These act like men who are still enjoying the pleasures of this world!' And they told the thing to the Blessed One.*"

Besides Tennōji, Ōsaka has many famous temples, both Buddhist and Shintō, with very

of the civil laws forbidding priests to marry. The wives of the priests of other sects than the Shinshū are called by a humorous and not very respectful appellation.

ancient histories. Of such is Kōzu-no-yashiro, where the people pray to the spirit of Nintoku, — most beloved in memory of all Japanese emperors. He had a palace on the same hill where his shrine now stands; and this site — whence a fine view of the city can be obtained — is the scene of a pleasing legend preserved in the Kojiki: —

. . . "Thereupon the Heavenly Sovereign, ascending a lofty mountain and looking on the land all round, spoke, saying: — 'In the whole land there rises no smoke; the land is all poverty-stricken. So I remit all the people's taxes and forced labor from now till three years hence.' Thereupon the great palace became dilapidated, and the rain leaked in everywhere; but no repairs were made. The rain that leaked in was caught in troughs, and the inmates removed to places where there was no leakage. When later the Heavenly Sovereign looked upon the land, the smoke was abundant in the land. So, finding the people rich, he now exacted taxes and forced labor. Therefore the peasantry prospered, and did not suffer from the forced labor. So, in praise of that august reign, it was called the Reign of the Emperor-Sage." [1]

[1] See Professor Chamberlain's translation of the Kojiki, section CXXI.

That was fifteen hundred years ago. Now, could the good Emperor see, from his shrine of Kōzu, — as thousands must believe he does, — the smoke of modern Ōsaka, he might well think, "My people are becoming too rich."

Outside of the city there is a still more famous Shintō temple, Sumiyoshi, dedicated to certain sea-gods who aided the Empress Jingō to conquer Korea. At Sumiyoshi there are pretty child-priestesses, and beautiful grounds, and an enormous pond spanned by a bridge so humped that, to cross it without taking off your shoes, you must cling to the parapet. At Sakai there is the Buddhist temple of Myōkokuji, in the garden of which are some very old palm-trees; — one of them, removed by Nobunaga in the sixteenth century, is said to have cried out and lamented until it was taken back to the temple. You see the ground under these palms covered with what looks like a thick, shiny, disordered mass of fur, — half reddish and half silvery grey. It is not fur. It is a heaping of millions of needles thrown there by pilgrims "to feed the palms," because these trees are said to love iron and to be strengthened by absorbing its rust.

Speaking of trees, I may mention the Naniwaya "Kasa-matsu," or Hat-Pine, — not so much because it is an extraordinary tree as because it supports a large family who keep a little tea-house on the road to Sakai. The branches of the tree have been trained outwards and downwards over a framework of poles, so that the whole presents the appearance of an enormous green hat of the shape worn by peasants and called Kasa. The pine is scarcely six feet high, but covers perhaps twenty square yards; — its trunk, of course, not being visible at all from outside the framework supporting the branches. Many people visit the house to look at the pine and drink a cup of tea; and nearly every visitor buys some memento of it, — perhaps a woodcut of the tree, or a printed copy of verses written by some poet in praise of it, or a girl's hairpin, the top of which is a perfect little green model of the tree, — framework of poles and all, — with one tiny stork perched on it. The owners of the Naniwaya, as their tea-house is called, are not only able to make a good living, but to educate their children, by the exhibition of this tree, and the sale of such mementos.

I do not intend to tax my reader's patience by descriptions of the other famous temples of Ōsaka, — several of which are enormously old, and have most curious legends attached to them. But I may venture a few words about the cemetery of the Temple of One Soul, — or better, perhaps, the Temple of a Single Mind: Isshinji. The monuments there are the most extraordinary I ever saw. Near the main gate is the tomb of a wrestler, — Asahigorō Hachirō. His name is chiseled upon a big disk of stone, probably weighing a ton; and this disk is supported on the back of a stone image of a wrestler, — a grotesque figure, with gilded eyes starting from their sockets, and features apparently distorted by effort. It is a very queer thing, — half-comical, half-furious of aspect. Close by is the tomb of one Hirayama Hambei, — a monument shaped like a *hyōtan*, — that is to say, like a wine-gourd such as travelers use for carrying saké. The most usual form of *hyōtan* resembles that of an hour-glass, except that the lower part is somewhat larger than the upper; and the vessel can only stand upright when full or partly full, — so that in a Japanese song the wine-lover is made to say to his gourd, "*With you I fall.*" Apparently the mighty to drink wine have a district all to themselves in this cemetery; for there are several other monuments of like form in the same row, — also one shaped like a very large saké-bottle (*isshōdokkuri*),[1] on which is inscribed a verse not taken from the sutras. But the oddest monument of all is a great stone badger, sitting upright, and seeming to strike its belly with its forepaws. On the belly is cut a name, Inouyé Dennosuké, together with the verse: —

> Tsuki yo yoshi
> Nembutsu tonaite
> Hara tsudzumi.

Which means about as follows: — "On fine moonlight-nights, repeating the Nembutsu, I play the belly-drum." The flower-vases are in the form of saké-bottles. Artificial rock-work supports the monument; and here and there,

[1] That is, a bottle containing one sho, — about a quart and a half.

among the rocks, are smaller figures of badgers, dressed like Buddhist priests (tanuki-bozu). My readers probably know that the Japanese tanuki [1] is credited with the power of assuming human shape, and of making musical sounds like the booming of a handdrum by tapping upon its belly. It is said often to disguise itself as a Buddhist priest for mischievous purposes, and to be very fond of saké. Of course, such images in a cemetery represent nothing more than eccentricities, and are judged to be in bad taste. One is reminded of certain jocose paintings and inscriptions upon Greek and Roman tombs, expressing in regard to death — or rather in regard to life — a sentiment, or an affectation of sentiment, repellent to modern feeling.

v

I said in a former essay that a Japanese city is little more than a wilderness of wooden sheds, and Ōsaka is no exception.

---

[1] Although *tanuki* is commonly translated by "badger," the creature so called is not a real badger, but a kind of fruit-fox. It is also termed the "raccoon-faced dog." The true badger is, however, also found in Japan.

But interiorly a very large number of the frail wooden dwellings of any Japanese city are works of art; and perhaps no city possesses more charming homes than Ōsaka. Kyōto is, indeed, much richer in gardens, — there being comparatively little space for gardens in Ōsaka; but I am speaking of the houses only. Exteriorly a Japanese street may appear little better than a row of wooden barns or stables, but the interior of any dwelling in it may be a wonder of beauty. Usually the outside of a Japanese house is not at all beautiful, though it may have a certain pleasing oddity of form; and in many cases the walls of the rear or sides are covered with charred boards, of which the blackened and hardened surfaces are said to resist heat and damp better than any coating of paint or stucco could do. Except, perhaps, the outside of a coal-shed, nothing dingier-looking could be imagined. But the other side of the black walls may be an æsthetic delight. The comparative cheapness of the residence does not much affect this possibility; — for the Japanese excel all nations in obtaining the maximum of beauty with the minimum of cost;

while the most industrially advanced of Western peoples — the practical Americans — have yet only succeeded in obtaining the minimum of beauty with the maximum of cost! Much about Japanese interiors can be learned from Morse's "Japanese Homes;" but even that admirable book gives only the black-and-white notion of the subject; and more than half of the charm of such interiors is the almost inexplicable caress of color. To illustrate Mr. Morse's work so as to interpret the colorific charm would be a dearer and a more difficult feat than the production of Racinet's "Costumes Historique." Even thus the subdued luminosity, the tone of perfect repose, the revelations of delicacy and daintiness waiting the eye in every nook of chambers seemingly contrived to catch and keep the feeling of perpetual summer, would remain unguessed. Five years ago I wrote that a little acquaintance with the Japanese art of flower arrangement had made it impossible for me to endure the sight of that vulgarity, or rather brutality, which in the West we call a "bouquet." To-day I must add that familiarity with Japanese interiors has equally disgusted me with

IN OSAKA

Occidental interiors, no matter how spacious or comfortable or richly furnished. Returning now to Western life, I should feel like Thomas-the-Rhymer revisiting a world of ugliness and sorrow after seven years of fairyland.

It is possible, as has been alleged (though I cannot believe it), that Western artists have little more to learn from the study of Japanese pictorial art. But I am quite sure that our house-builders have universes of facts to learn — especially as regards the treatment and tinting of surfaces — from the study of Japanese interiors. Whether the countless styles of these interiors can even be classed appears to me a doubtful question. I do not think that in a hundred thousand Japanese houses there are two interiors precisely alike — (excluding, of course, the homes of the poorest classes), — for the designer never repeats himself when he can help it. The lesson he has to teach is the lesson of perfect taste combined with inexhaustible variety. Taste! — what a rare thing it is in our Western world! — and how independent of material, — how intuitive, — how incommunicable to the vulgar! But taste is a Japanese birthright.

It is everywhere present, — though varying in quality of development according to conditions and the inheritance depending upon conditions. The average Occidental recognizes only the commoner forms of it, — chiefly those made familiar by commercial export. And, as a general rule, what the West most admires in Japanese conventional taste is thought rather vulgar in Japan. Not that we are wrong in admiring whatever is beautiful in itself. Even the designs printed in tints upon a two-cent towel may be really great pictures: they are sometimes made by excellent artists. But the aristocratic severity of the best Japanese taste — the exquisite complexity of its refinements in the determination of proportion, quality, tone, restraint — has never yet been dreamed of by the West. Nowhere is this taste so finely exhibited as in private interiors, — particularly in regard to color. The rules of color in the composition of a set of rooms are not less exacting than the rules of color in the matter of dress, — though permitting considerable variety. The mere tones of a private house are enough to indicate its owner's degree of culture. There is no painting, no varnishing, no wall-papering, — only staining and polishing of particular parts, and a sort of paper border about fifteen inches broad fixed along the bottom of a wall to protect it during cleaning and dusting operations. The plastering may be made with sands of different hues, or with fragments of shell and nacre, or with quartz-crystal, or with mica; the surface may imitate granite, or may sparkle like copper pyrites, or may look exactly like a rich mass of bark; but, whatever the material, the tint given must show the same faultless taste that rules in the tints of silks for robes and girdles. . . . As yet, all this interior world of beauty — just because it is an interior world — is closed to the foreign tourist: he can find at most only suggestions of it in the rooms of such old-fashioned inns or tea-houses as he may visit in the course of his travels.

I wonder how many foreign travelers understand the charm of a Japanese inn, or even think how much is done to please them, not merely in the matter of personal attentions, but in making beauty for their eyes. Multitudes write of their petty vexations, — their personal acquaintance with fleas, their personal dislikes and discomforts; but how many write of the charm of that alcove where every day fresh flowers are placed, — arranged as no European florist could ever learn to arrange flowers, — and where there is sure to be some object of real art, whether in bronze, lacquer, or porcelain, together with a picture suited to the feeling of the time and season? These little æsthetic gratifications, though never charged for, ought to be kindly remembered when the gift of "tea-money" is made. I have been in hundreds of Japanese hotels, and I remember only one in which I could find nothing curious or pretty, — a ramshackle shelter hastily put up to catch custom at a newly-opened railway station.

A word about the alcove of my room in Ōsaka: — The wall was covered only with a mixture of sand and metallic filings of some sort, but it looked like a beautiful surface of silver ore. To the pillar was fastened a bamboo cup containing a pair of exquisite blossoming sprays of wistaria, — one pink and the other white. The kakemono — made with a few very bold strokes by a master-brush — pictured two enormous crabs about to fight after vainly trying to get out of each other's way; — and the humor of the thing was enhanced by a few Chinese characters signifying, *Wōko-sekai*, or, "Everything goes crookedly in this world."

VII

My last day in Ōsaka was given to shopping, — chiefly in the districts of the toy-makers and of the silk merchants. A Japanese acquaintance, himself a shopkeeper, took me about, and showed me extraordinary things until my eyes ached. We went to a famous silk-house, — a tumultuous place, so crowded that we had some trouble to squeeze our way to the floor-platform, which, in every Japanese shop, serves at once for chairs and counter. Scores of barefooted light-limbed boys were running over it, bearing bundles of merchandise to customers; — for in such shops there is no shelving of stock. The Japanese salesman never leaves his squatting-place on the mats; but, on learning what you want, he shouts an order, and boys presently run to you with armfuls of samples. After you have made your choice, the goods are rolled up again by the boys, and carried back into the fire-proof storehouses behind the shop. At the time of our visit, the greater part of the matted floor-space was one splendid shimmering confusion of tossed silks and velvets of a hundred colors and a hundred prices. Near the main entrance an elderly superintendent, plump and jovial of aspect like the God of Wealth, looked after arriving customers. Two keen-eyed men, standing upon an elevation in the middle of the shop, and slowly turning round and round in opposite directions, kept watch for thieves; and other watchers were posted at the side-doors. (Japanese shop-thieves, by the way, are very clever; and I am told that nearly every large store loses considerably by them in the course of the year.) In a side-wing of the building, under a low skylight, I saw busy ranks of bookkeepers, cashiers, and correspondents squatting before little desks less than two feet high. Each of the numerous salesmen was attending to many customers at once. The rush of business was big; and the rapidity with which the work was being done testified

IN OSAKA

to the excellence of the organization established. I asked how many persons the firm employed, and my friend replied: —

"Probably about two hundred here; there are several branch houses. In this shop the work is very hard; but the working-hours are shorter than in most of the silk-houses, — not more than twelve hours a day."

"What about salaries?" I inquired.

"No salaries."

"Is all the work of this firm done without pay?"

"Perhaps one or two of the very cleverest salesmen may get something, — not exactly a salary, but a little special remuneration every month; and the old superintendent — (he has been forty years in the house) — gets a salary. The rest get nothing but their food."

"Good food?"

"No, very cheap, coarse food. After a man has served his time here, — fourteen or fifteen years, — he may be helped to open a small store of his own."

"Are the conditions the same in all the shops of Ōsaka?"

"Yes, — everywhere the same. But now

many of the detchi are graduates of commercial schools. Those sent to a commercial school begin their apprenticeship much later; and they are said not to make such good detchi as those taught from childhood."

"A Japanese clerk in a foreign store is much better off."

"We do not think so," answered my friend very positively. "Some who speak English well, and have learned the foreign way of doing business, may get fifty or sixty dollars a month for seven or eight hours' work a day. But they are not treated the same way as they are treated in a Japanese house. Clever men do not like to work under foreigners. Foreigners used to be very cruel to their Japanese clerks and servants."

"But not now?" I queried.

"Perhaps not often. They have found that it is dangerous. But they used to beat and kick them. Japanese think it shameful to even speak unkindly to detchi or servants. In a house like this there is no unkindness. The owners and the superintendents never speak roughly. You see how very hard all these men and boys are working without pay.

No foreigner could get Japanese to work like that, even for big wages. I have worked in foreign houses, and I know."

It is not exaggeration to say that most of the intelligent service rendered in Japanese trade and skilled industry is unsalaried. Perhaps one third of the business work of the country is done without wages; the relation between master and servant being one of perfect trust on both sides, and absolute obedience being assured by the simplest of moral conditions. This fact was the fact most deeply impressed upon me during my stay in Ōsaka.

I found myself wondering about it while the evening train to Nara was bearing me away from the cheery turmoil of the great metropolis. I continued to think of it while watching the deepening of the dusk over the leagues of roofs, — over the mustering of factory chimneys forever sending up their offering of smoke to the shrine of good Nintoku. Suddenly above the out-twinkling of countless lamps, — above the white star-points of electric lights, — above the growing dusk itself, — I saw, rising glorified into the last red splendor of sunset, the marvelous old pagoda of Tennōji. And I asked myself whether the faith it symbolized had not helped to create that spirit of patience and love and trust upon which have been founded all the wealth and energy and power of the mightiest city of Japan.

VIII

BUDDHIST ALLUSIONS IN JAPANESE FOLK-SONG

PERHAPS only a Japanese representative of the older culture could fully inform us to what degree the mental soil of the race has been saturated and fertilized by Buddhist idealism. At all events, no European could do so; for to understand the whole relation of Far-Eastern religion to Far-Eastern life would require, not only such scholarship, but also such experience as no European could gain in a lifetime. Yet for even the Western stranger there are everywhere signs of what Buddhism has been to Japan in the past. All the arts and most of the industries repeat Buddhist legends to the eye trained in symbolism; and there is scarcely an object of handiwork possessing any beauty or significance of form — from the plaything of a child to the heirloom of a prince — which does not in some way proclaim the ancient debt to Buddhism of the craft that made it. One may discern Buddhist thoughts in the cheap cotton prints from an Ōsaka mill not less than in the figured silks of Kyōto. The reliefs upon an iron kettle, or the elephant-heads of bronze making the handles of a shopkeeper's *hibachi;* — the patterns of screen-paper, or the commonest ornamental woodwork of a gateway; — the etchings upon a metal pipe, or the enameling upon a costly vase, — may all relate, with equal eloquence, the traditions of faith. There are reflections or echoes of Buddhist teaching in the composition of a garden; — in the countless ideographs of the long vistas of shop-signs; — in the wonderfully expressive names given to certain fruits and flowers; — in the appellations of mountains, capes, waterfalls, villages, — even of modern railway stations. And the new civilization would not yet seem to have much affected the influence thus manifested. Trains and steamers now yearly carry to famous shrines more pilgrims than visited them ever before in a twelvemonth; — the temple bells still, in despite of clocks and watches, mark

IN JAPANESE FOLK-SONG 187

the passing of time for the millions; — the speech of the people is still poetized with Buddhist utterances; — literature and drama still teem with Buddhist expressions; — and the most ordinary voices of the street — songs of children playing, a chorus of laborers at their toil, even cries of itinerant street-venders — often recall to me some story of saints and Bodhisattvas, or the text of some sutra.

Such an experience first gave me the idea of making a collection of songs containing Buddhist expressions or allusions. But in view of the extent of the subject I could not at once decide where to begin. A bewildering variety of Japanese songs — a variety of which the mere nomenclature would occupy pages — offers material of this description. Among noteworthy kinds may be mentioned the *Utai*, dramatic songs, mostly composed by high priests, of which probably no ten lines are without some allusion to Buddhism; — the *Naga-uta*, songs often of extraordinary length; — and the *Jōruri*, whole romances in verse, with which professional singers can delight their audiences for five or six hours at a time. The mere dimension of such compositions necessarily excluded them from my plan; but there remained a legion of briefer forms to choose among. I resolved at last to limit my undertaking mainly to *dodoitsu*, — little songs of twenty-six syllables only, arranged in four lines (7, 7, 7, 5). They are more regular in construction than the street-songs treated of in a former paper; but they are essentially popular, and therefore more widely representative of Buddhist influences than many superior kinds of composition could be. Out of a very large number collected for me, I have selected between forty and fifty as typical of the class.

Perhaps those pieces which reflect the ideas of preëxistence and of future rebirths will prove especially interesting to the Western reader, — much less because of poetical worth than because of comparative novelty. We have very little English verse of any class containing fancies of this kind; but they swarm in Japanese poetry even as commonplaces and conventionalisms. Such an exquisite thing as Rossetti's "Sudden Light," — bewitching us chiefly through the penetrative subtlety of a thought anathematized by all our orthodoxies for eighteen hundred years, — could interest a Japanese only as the exceptional rendering, by an Occidental, of fancies and feelings familiar to the most ignorant peasant. Certainly no one will be able to find in these Japanese verses — or, rather, in my own wretchedly prosy translations of them — even a hint of anything like the ghostly delicacy of Rossetti's imagining : —

> I have been here before, —
>   But when or how I cannot tell :
> I know the grass beyond the door,
>   The sweet, keen smell,
> The sighing sound, the lights along the shore.

> You have been mine before, —
>   How long ago I may not know :
> But just when at that swallow's soar
>   Your neck turned so,
> Some veil did fall, — I knew it all of yore.

Yet what a queer *living* difference between such enigmatically delicate handling of thoughts classed as forbidden fruit in the Western Eden of Dreams and the every-day Japanese utterances that spring directly out of ancient Eastern faith ! —

Love, it is often said, has nothing to do with reason.
The cause of ours must be some En *in a previous birth.*[1]

Even the knot of the rope tying our boats together
Knotted was long ago by some love in a former birth.

If the touching even of sleeves be through En *of a former existence,*
Very much deeper must be the En *that unites us now!* [2]

Kwahō [3] *this life must be,— this dwelling with one so tender;—*
I am reaping now the reward of deeds in a former birth!

> [1] Iro wa shian no
>   Hoka to-wa iédo,
>   Koré mo saki-sho no
>   En de arō.

"En" is a Buddhist word signifying affinity,— relation of cause and effect from life to life.

> [2] Sodé suri-ō no mo
>   Tashō no en yo,
>   Mashité futari ga
>   Fukai naka.

Allusion is here made to the old Buddhist proverb: *Sodé no furi-awasé mo tashō no en,* — "Even the touching of sleeves in passing is caused by some affinity operating from former lives."

[3] The Buddhist word "Kwahō" is commonly used instead of other synonyms for Karma (such as ingwa, innen, etc.), to signify the good, rather than the bad results of action in previous lives. But it is sometimes used in both meanings. Here there seems to be an allusion to the proverbial expression, *Kwahō no yoi hito* (lit.: **a person of good Kwahō**), meaning a fortunate individual.

Many songs of this class refer to the customary vow which lovers make to belong to each other for more lives than one, — a vow perhaps originally inspired by the Buddhist aphorism, —

> *Oya-ko wa, is-sé;*
> *Fūfu wa, ni-sé;*
> *Shujū wa, san-zé.*

"The relation of parent and child is for one life; that of wife and husband, for two lives; that of master and servant, for three lives." Although the tender relation is thus limited to the time of two lives, the vow — (as Japanese dramas testify, and as the letters of those who kill themselves for love bear witness) — is often passionately made for seven. The following selections show a considerable variety of tone, — ranging from the pathetic to the satirical, — in the treatment of this topic:

I have cut my hair for his sake; but the deeper relation between us
Cannot be cut in this, nor yet in another life. [1]

> [1] Kami wa kitté mo
> Ni-sé madé kaketa
> Fukai enishi wa
> Kiru mono ka?
>
> Literally: "Hair have-cut although, two existences until,

*She looks at the portrait of him to whom for two lives she is
  promised:*
*Happy remembrances come, and each brings a smile to her
  face.*[1]

*If in this present life we never can hope for union,
Then we shall first keep house in the Lotos-Palace beyond.*[2]

*Have we not spoken the vow that binds for a double existence?
If we must separate now, I can only wish to die.*

deep relation, cut-how-can-it-be?" By the mention of the
hair-cutting we know the speaker is a woman. Her husband, or possibly betrothed lover, is dead; and, according
to the Buddhist custom, she signifies her desire to remain
faithful to his memory by the sacrifice of her hair. For
detailed information on this subject see, in my *Glimpses of
Unfamiliar Japan*, the chapter, "Of Women's Hair."

[1] Ni-sé to chigirishi
    Shashin wo nagamé
    Omoi-idashité
    Warai-gao.

Lit.: "Two existences that made alliance, photograph
look-at, thinking bring-out smiling face." The use of the
term *shashin*, photograph, shows that the poem is not old.

[2] Totémo kono yo dé
    Sowaré-nu naraba
    Hasu no uténa dé
    Ara sétai.

Lit.: "By-any-means, this-world-in, cannot-live-together
if, Lotos-of Palace-in, new-housekeeping." It is with this
thought that lovers voluntarily die together; and the song
might be called a song of *jōshi*.

There! — oh, what shall we do? . . . Pledged for a double existence, —
And now, as we sit together, the string of the samisen snaps! [1]

He woos by teaching the Law of Cause and Effect for three lives,
And makes a contract for two — the crafty-smiling priest! [2]

Every mortal has lived and is destined to live countless lives; yet the happy moments of any single existence are not therefore less precious in themselves: —

Not to have met one night is verily cause for sorrow;
Since twice in a single birth the same night never comes.

But even as a summer unusually warm is apt to herald a winter of exceptional severity, so too much happiness in this life may signify great suffering in the next: —

Always I suffer thus! . . . Methinks, in my last existence,
Too happy I must have been, — did not suffer enough.

Next in point of exotic interest to the songs expressing belief in preëxistence and rebirth, I think I should place those treating of the

---

[1] Among singing-girls it is believed that the snapping of a samisen-string under such circumstances as those indicated in the above song is an omen of coming separation.

[2] This song is of a priest who breaks the vow of celibacy.

doctrine of *ingwa*, or Karma. I offer some free translations from these, together with one selection from a class of compositions more elaborate and usually much longer than the *dodoitsu*, called *hauta*. In the original, at least, my selection from the *hauta* — which contains a charming simile about the firefly — is by far the prettiest: —

Weep not! — turn to me! . . . Nay, all my suspicions vanish!
Forgive me those words unkind: some ingwa *controlled my tongue!*

Evidently this is the remorseful pleading of a jealous lover. The next might be the answer of the girl whose tears he had caused to flow:

I cannot imagine at all by what strange manner of ingwa
Came I to fall in love with one so unkind as you!

Or she might exclaim: —

Is this the turning of En? *— am I caught in the Wheel of Karma?*
That, alas! is a wheel not to be moved from the rut![1]

[1] Meguru en kaya?
Kuruma no watashi
Hiku ni hikarénu
Kono ingwa.

There is a play on words in the original which I have not attempted to render. The idea is of an unhappy match —

A more remarkable reference to the Wheel of Karma is the following: —

Father and mother forbade, and so I gave up my lover; —
Yet still, with the whirl of the Wheel, the thought of him comes and goes.[1]

This is a *hauta* : —

Numberless insects there are that call from dawn to evening,
Crying, " I love ! I love ! " — but the Firefly's silent passion,
Making its body burn, is deeper than all their longing.
Even such is my love . . . yet I cannot think through what ingwa
I opened my heart — alas ! — to a being not sincere ![2]

either betrothal or marriage — from which the woman wishes to withdraw when too late.

[1] Oya no iken dé
 Akirameta no wo
 Mata mo rin-yé dé
  Omoi-dasu.

The Buddhist word *Rin-yé*, or *Rinten*, has the meaning of "turning the Wheel," — another expression for passing from birth to birth. The Wheel here is the great Circle of Illusion, — the whirl of Karma.

[2] Kaäi, kaäi to
 Naku mushi yori mo
 Nakanu hotaru ga
 Mi wo kogasu.
 Nanno ingwa dé
 Jitsu naki hito ni
 Shin wo akashité, —
  Aa kuyashi!

Lit.: " ' I-love-I-love '-saying-cry-insects than, better

If the foregoing seem productions possible only to our psychological antipodes, it is quite otherwise with a group of folk-songs reflecting the doctrine of Impermanency. Concerning the instability of all material things, and the hollowness of all earthly pleasures, Christian and Buddhist thought are very much in accord. The great difference between them appears only when we compare their teaching as to things ghostly, — and especially as to the nature of the Ego. But the Oriental doctrine that the Ego itself is an impermanent compound, and that the Self is not the true Consciousness, rarely finds expression in these popular songs. For the common people the Self exists: it is a real (though multiple) personality that passes from birth to birth. Only the educated Buddhist comprehends the deeper teaching that what we imagine to be Self is wholly illusion, — a darkening veil woven by Karma; and that there is no Self but the Infinite Self, the eternal Absolute.

---

never-cry-firefly, body scorch! What Karma because-of, sincerity-not-is-man to, inmost-mind opened? — ah! regret!" . . . It was formerly believed that the firefly's light really burned its own body.

In the following *dodoitsu* will be found mostly thoughts or emotions according with universal experience: —

Gathering clouds to the moon; — storm and rain to the flowers:
Somehow this world of woe never is just as we like.[1]

Almost as soon as they bloom, the scented flowers of the plum-tree
By the wind of this world of change are scattered and blown away.

Thinking to-morrow remains, thou heart's frail flower-of-cherry?
How knowest whether this night the tempest will not come?[2]

[1] Tsuki ni murakumo,
   Hana ni wa arashi:
   Tokaku uki-yo wa
      Mama naranu.

This song especially refers to unhappy love, and contains the substance of two Buddhist proverbs: *Tsuki ni murakumo, hana ni kazé* (cloud-masses to the moon; wind to flowers); and *Mama ni naranu wa uki-yo no narai* (to be disappointed is the rule in this miserable world). "Uki-yo" (this fleeting or unhappy world) is one of the commonest Buddhist terms in use.

[2] Asu ari to
   Omō kokoro no
      Ada-zakura:
   Yo wa ni arashi no
      Fukanu monokawa?

Lit.: "To-morrow-is that think heart-of perishable-cherry flower: this-night-in-storm blow-not, is-it-certain?"

Shadow and shape alike melt and flow back to nothing:
He who knows this truth is the Daruma of snow.[1]

As the moon of the fifteenth night, the heart till the age fifteen:
Then the brightness wanes, and the darkness comes with love.[2]

All things change, we are told, in this world of change and sorrow;
But love's way never changes of promising never to change.[3]

[1] Kagé mo katachi mo
Kiyuréba moto no
Midzu to satoru zo
Yuki-Daruma.

Lit.: "Shadow and shape also, if-melt-away, original-water is, — that-understands Snow-Daruma." Daruma (Dharma), the twenty-eighth patriarch of the Zen sect, is said to have lost his legs through remaining long in the posture of meditation; and many legless toy-figures, which are so balanced that they will always assume an upright position however often placed upside-down, are called by his name. The snow-men made by Japanese children have the same traditional form. — The Japanese friend who helped me to translate these verses, tells me that a ghostly meaning attaches to the word "Kagé" [shadow] in the above; — this would give a much more profound signification to the whole verse.

[2] According to the old calendar, there was always a full moon on the fifteenth of the month. The Buddhist allusion in the verse is to *mayoi*, the illusion of passion, which is compared to a darkness concealing the Right Way.

[3] Kawaru uki-yo ni
Kawaranu mono wa

Cruel the beautiful flash, — utterly heartless that lightning!
Before one can look even twice it vanishes wholly away! [1]

His very sweetness itself makes my existence a burden!
Truly this world of change is a world of constant woe! [2]

Neither for youth nor age is fixed the life of the body; —
Bidding me wait for a time is the word that forever divides. [3]

> Kawarumai to no
> Koi no michi.

Lit.: "Change changeable-world-in, does-not-change that-which, 'We-will-never-change'-saying of Love-of Way."

[1] Honni tsurénai
Ano inadzuma wa
Futa mé minu uchi
Kiyété yuku.

The Buddhist saying, *Inadzuma no hikari, ishi no hi* (lightning-flash and flint-spark), — symbolizing the temporary nature of all pleasures, — is here playfully referred to. The song complains of a too brief meeting with sweetheart or lover.

[2] Words of a loving but jealous woman, thus interpreted by my Japanese friend: "The more kind he is, the more his kindness overwhelms me with anxiety lest he be equally tender to other girls who may also fall in love with him."

[3] Rō-shō fujō no
Mi dé ari nagara,
Jisetsu maté to wa
Kiré-kotoba.

Lit.: "Old-young not-fixed-of body being, time-wait to-say, cutting-word." "Ros-hō fujō" is a Buddhist phrase. The meaning of the song is: "Since all things in this

Only too well I know that to meet will cause more weeping; [1]
Yet never to meet at all were sorrow too great to bear.

Too joyful in union to think, we forget that the smiles of the evening
Sometimes themselves become the sources of morning-tears.

Yet, notwithstanding the doctrine of impermanency, we are told in another *dodoitsu* that —

He who was never bewitched by the charming smile of a woman,
A wooden Buddha is he — a Buddha of bronze or stone! [2]

And why a Buddha of wood, or bronze, or stone? Because the living Buddha was not

world are uncertain, asking me to wait for our marriage-day means that you do not really love me; — for either of us might die before the time you speak of."

[1] Allusion is made to the Buddhist text, *Shōja hitsu metsu, esha jō ri* ("Whosoever is born must die, and all who meet must as surely part"), and to the religious phrase, *Ai betsu ri ku* ("Sorrow of parting and pain of separation").

[2] Much more amusing in the original: —

> Adana é-gao ni
> Mayowanu mono wa
> Ki-Butsu, — kana-Butsu, —
> Ishi-botoké!

"Charming-smile-by bewildered-not, he-as-for, wood-Buddha, metal-Buddha, stone-Buddha!" The term "Ishi-botoké" especially refers to the stone images of the Buddha so insensible, as we are assured, with jocose irreverence, in the following: —

"Forsake this fitful world"! —
that was { *Lord Buddha's or upside-down* } *teaching!*
And Ragora,[1] son of his loins? — was he forgotten indeed?

There is an untranslatable pun in the original, which, if written in Romaji, would run thus: —

Uki-yo wo sutéyo t'a
Sorya { Shaka Sama / saka-sama } yo:
Ragora to iū ko wo
 Wasurété ka?

Shakamuni is the Japanese rendering of "Sakyamuni;" "Shaka Sama" is therefore "Lord Sakya," or "Lord Buddha." But *saka-sama* is a Japanese word meaning "topsy-turvy," "upside down;" and the difference between the pronunciation of Shaka Sama and *saka-sama* is slight enough to have suggested the pun. Love in suspense is not usually inclined to reverence.

placed in cemeteries. — This song is sung in every part of Japan; I have heard it many times in different places.

[1] *Râhula.*

Even while praying together in front of the tablets ancestral,
Lovers find chance to murmur prayers never meant for the dead ! [1]

And as for interrupters : —

Hateful the wind or rain that ruins the bloom of flowers:
Even more hateful far who obstructs the way of love.

Yet the help of the Gods is earnestly besought: —

I make my hyaku-dō, *traveling Love's dark pathway,*
Ever praying to meet the owner of my heart.[2]

---

[1] Ekō suru toté
   Hotoké no maé yé
   Futari mukaité,
      Konabé daté.

Lit.: "Repeat prayers saying, dead-of-presence-in twain facing, — small-pan cooking!" *Hotoké* means a dead person as well as a Buddha. (See my *Glimpses of Unfamiliar Japan:* "The Household Shrine"). *Konabé-daté* is an idiomatic expression signifying a lovers' tête-à-tête. It is derived from the phrase, *Chin-chin kamo nabé* ("cooking a wild duck in a pan"), — the idea suggested being that of the pleasure experienced by an amorous couple in eating out of the same dish. *Chin-chin,* an onomatope, expresses the sound of the gravy boiling.

[2] To perform the rite called "o-hyaku-dō" means to make one hundred visits to a temple, saying a prayer each time. The expression "dark way of Love" (*koi no yami* or *yamiji*) is a Buddhist phrase; love, being due to *mayoi, or*

The interest attaching to the following typical group of love-songs will be found to depend chiefly upon the Buddhist allusions: —

In the bed of the River of Souls, or in waiting alone at evening,
The pain differs nothing at all: to a mountain the pebble grows.[1]

Who furthest after illusion wanders on Love's dark pathway
Is ever the clearest-seeing,[2] *not the simple or dull.*

illusion, is a state of spiritual darkness. The term "owner of my heart" is an attempted rendering of the Japanese word *nushi*, signifying "master," "owner," — often, also, "landlord," — and, in love-matters, the lord or master of the affection inspired.

[1] Sai-no-kawara to
Nushi matsu yoi wa
Koishi, koishi ga
Yama to naru.

A more literal translation would be: "In the Sai-no-Kawara ('Dry bed of the River of Souls') and in the evening when waiting for the loved one, '*Koishi, Koishi*' becomes a mountain." There is a delicate pun here, — a play on the word *Koishi*, which, as pronounced, though not as written, may mean either "a small stone," or "longing to see." In the bed of the phantom river, Sai-no-Kawa, the ghosts of children are obliged to pile up little stones, the weight of which increases so as to tax their strength to the utmost. There is a reference here also to a verse in the Buddhist *wasan* of Jizō, describing the crying of the children for their parents: "*Chichi koishi! haha koishi!*" (See *Glimpses of Unfamiliar Japan*, vol. i. pp. 59-61.)

[2] Clearest-sighted, — that is, in worldly matters.

Coldly seen from without our love looks utter folly:
Who never has felt mayoi *never could understand!*

Countless the men must be who dwell in three thousand worlds;
Yet among them all is none worthy to change for mine.[1]

However fickle I seem, my heart is never unfaithful:
Out of the slime itself, spotless the lotos grows.[2]

So that we stay together, even the Hell of the Blood Lake —
Even the Mountain of Swords — will signify nothing at all.[3]

[1] San-zen sékai ni
 Otoko wa arédo,
 Nushi ni mi-kayeru
 Hito wa nai.

"San-zen sekai," the three thousand worlds, is a common Buddhist expression. Literally translated, the above song runs: "Three-thousand-worlds-in men are, but lover-to-exchange person is not."

[2] The familiar Buddhist simile is used more significantly here than the Western reader might suppose from the above rendering. These are supposed to be the words either of a professional singing-girl or of a *jorō*. Her calling is derisively termed a *doro-midzu kagyō* ("foul-water occupation"); and her citation of the famous Buddhist comparison in self-defense is particularly, and pathetically, happy.

[3] Chi-no-Iké-Jigoku mo,
 Tsurugi-no-Yama mo,
 Futari-dzuré nara
 Itoi 'a sénu.

The Hell of the Blood-Lake is a hell for women; and the Mountain of Swords is usually depicted in Buddhist

Not yet indeed is my body garbed in the ink-black habit; —
But as for this heart bereaved, already it is a nun.[1]

My hair, indeed, is uncut; but my heart has become a religious;
A nun it shall always be till the hour I meet him again.

But even the priest or nun is not always exempt from the power of *mayoi*: —

I am wearing the sable garb, — and yet, through illusion of longing,
Ever I lose my way, — knowing not whither or where!

So far, my examples have been principally chosen from the more serious class of *dodoitsu*. But in *dodoitsu* of a lighter class the Buddhist allusions are perhaps even more frequent. The following group of five will serve for specimens of hundreds: —

prints as a place of infernal punishment for men in especial.

[1] In the original much more pretty and much more simple: —

>   Sumi no koromo ni
>   Mi wa yatsusanedo,
>   Kokoro hitotsu wa
>   Ama-hōshi.

"Ink-black-*koromo* [priest's or nun's outer robe] in, body not clad, but heart-one nun." *Hitotsu*, "one," also means "solitary," "forlorn," "bereaved." *Ama hōshi*, lit.: "nun-priest."

Never can be recalled the word too quickly spoken:
Therefore with Emma's face the lover receives the prayer.[1]

Thrice did I hear that prayer with Buddha's face; but hereafter
My face shall be Emma's face because of too many prayers.

Now they are merry together; but under their boat is Jigoku.[2]
Blow quickly, thou river-wind, — blow a typhoon for my sake!

Vainly, to make him stay, I said that the crows were night crows;[3] —
The bell of the dawn peals doom, — the bell that cannot lie.

---

[1] The implication is that he has hastily promised more than he wishes to perform. Emma, or Yemma (Sansc. Yama), is the Lord of Hell and Judge of Souls; and, as depicted in Buddhist sculpture and painting, is more than fearful to look upon. There is an evident reference in this song to the Buddhist proverb: *Karu-toki no Jizō-gao; nasu-toki no Emma-gao* ("Borrowing-time, the face of Jizō; repaying-time, the face of Emma").

[2] "Jigoku" is the Buddhist name for various hells (Sansc. *narakas*). The allusion here is to the proverb, *Funa-ita ichi-mai shita wa Jigoku:* "Under [*the thickness of*] a single boat-plank is hell," — referring to the perils of the sea. This song is a satire on jealousy; and the boat spoken of is probably a roofed pleasure-boat, such as excursions are made into the sound of music.

[3] *Tsuki-yo-garasu*, lit.: "moon-night crows." Crows usually announce the dawn by their cawing; but sometimes on moonlight nights they caw at all hours from sunset to sun-

*This my desire: To kill the crows of three thousand worlds,
And then to repose in peace with the owner of my heart!* [1]

I have cited this last only as a curiosity. For it has a strange history, and is not what it seems, — although the apparent motive was certainly suggested by some song like the one immediately preceding it. It is a song of loyalty, and was composed by Kido of Chōshū, one of the leaders in that great movement which brought about the downfall of the Shōgunate, the restoration of the Imperial power, the reconstruction of Japanese society, and the introduction and adoption of Western civilization. Kido, Saigō, and Ōkubo are rightly termed the three heroes of the restoration. While preparing his plans at Kyōto, in company with his friend Saigō, Kido com-

---

rise. The bell referred to is the bell of some Buddhist temple: the *aké-no-kane*, or "dawn-bell," being, in all parts of Japan, sounded from every Buddhist *tera*. There is a pun in the original; — the expression *tsukenai*, "cannot *tell* [a lie]," might also be interpreted phonetically as "cannot *strike* [a bell]."

[1] San-zen sékai no
Karasu wo koroshi
Nushi to soi-né ga
Shité mitai!

posed and sang this song as an intimation of his real sentiments. By the phrase, "ravens of the three thousand worlds," he designated the Tokugawa partisans; by the word *nushi* (lord, or heart's-master) he signified the Emperor; and by the term *soiné* (reposing together) he referred to the hoped-for condition of direct responsibility to the Throne, without further intervention of Shōgun and daimyō. It was not the first example in Japanese history of the use of popular song as a medium for the utterance of opinions which, expressed in plainer language, would have invited assassination.

While I was writing the preceding note upon Kido's song, the Buddhist phrase, *Sanzen sékai* (twice occurring, as the reader will have observed, in the present collection), suggested a few reflections with which this paper may fitly conclude. I remember that when I first attempted, years ago, to learn the outlines of Buddhist philosophy, one fact which particularly impressed me was the vastness of the Buddhist concept of the universe. Buddhism, as I read it, had not offered itself to humanity as a saving creed for one inhabited world, but as the religion of "innumerable hundreds of thousands of myriads of *kôtis* [1] of worlds." And the modern scientific revelation of stellar evolution and dissolution then seemed to me, and still seems, like a prodigious confirmation of certain Buddhist theories of cosmical law.

The man of science to-day cannot ignore the enormous suggestions of the new story that the heavens are telling. He finds himself compelled to regard the development of what we call mind as a general phase or incident in the ripening of planetary life throughout the universe. He is obliged to consider the relation of our own petty sphere to the great swarming of suns and systems as no more than the relation of a single noctiluca to the phosphorescence of a sea. By its creed the Oriental intellect has been better prepared than the Occidental to accept this tremendous revelation, not as a wisdom that increaseth sorrow, but as a wisdom to quicken faith. And I cannot but think that out of the certain future union of Western knowledge

[1] 1 kôti = 10,000,000.

with Eastern thought there must eventually proceed a Neo-Buddhism inheriting all the strength of Science, yet spiritually able to recompense the seeker after truth with the recompense foretold in the twelfth chapter of the Sutra of the Diamond-Cutter. Taking the text as it stands, — in despite of commentators, — what more could be unselfishly desired from any spiritual teaching than the reward promised in that verse, — "*They shall be endowed with the Highest Wonder*"?

IX

NIRVANA

A STUDY IN SYNTHETIC BUDDHISM

I

"It is not possible, O Subhûti, that this treatise of the Law should be heard by beings of little faith, — by those who believe in Self, in beings, in living beings, and in persons." — *The Diamond-Cutter*.

THERE still widely prevails in Europe and America the idea that Nirvana signifies, to Buddhist minds, neither more nor less than absolute nothingness, — complete annihilation. This idea is erroneous. But it is erroneous only because it contains half of a truth. This half of a truth has no value or interest, or even intelligibility, unless joined with the other half. And of the other half no suspicion yet exists in the average Western mind.

Nirvana, indeed, signifies an extinction. But if by this extinction of individual being we understand soul-death, our conception of Nirvana is wrong. Or if we take Nirvana to mean such reabsorption of the finite into the infinite as that predicted by Indian pantheism, again our idea is foreign to Buddhism.

Nevertheless, if we declare that Nirvana means the extinction of individual sensation, emotion, thought, — the final disintegration of conscious personality, — the annihilation of everything that can be included under the term "I," — then we rightly express one side of the Buddhist teaching.

The apparent contradiction of the foregoing statements is due only to our Occidental notion of Self. Self to us signifies feelings, ideas, memory, volition; and it can scarcely occur to any person not familiar with German idealism even to imagine that consciousness might not be Self. The Buddhist, on the contrary, declares all that we call Self to be false. He defines the Ego as a mere temporary aggregate of sensations, impulses, ideas, created by the physical and mental experiences of the race, — all related to the perishable body, and all doomed to dissolve with it. What to Western reasoning seems the most indubitable of realities, Buddhist reasoning pronounces the greatest of all illusions, and even the source of all sorrow and sin. "*The mind, the thoughts, and all the senses are subject to the law of life and death. With knowledge of Self and the laws of birth and death, there is no grasping, and no sense-perception. Knowing one's self and knowing how the senses act, there is no room for the idea of 'I,' or the ground for framing it. The thought of 'Self' gives rise to all sorrows, — binding the world as with fetters; but having found there is no ' I ' that can be bound, then all these bonds are severed.*"[1]

The above text suggests very plainly that the consciousness is not the Real Self, and that the mind dies with the body. Any reader unfamiliar with Buddhist thought may well ask, " What, then, is the meaning of the doctrine of Karma, the doctrine of moral progression, the doctrine of the consequence of acts ? " Indeed, to try to study, only with the ontological ideas of the West, even such translations of the Buddhist Sutras as those given in the " Sacred Books of the East," is to be

[1] *Fo-Sho-Hing-Tsan-King.*

at every page confronted by seemingly hopeless riddles and contradictions. We find a doctrine of rebirth; but the existence of a soul is denied. We are told that the misfortunes of this life are punishments of faults committed in a previous life; yet personal transmigration does not take place. We find the statement that beings are reindividualized; yet both individuality and personality are called illusions. I doubt whether anybody not acquainted with the deeper forms of Buddhist belief could possibly understand the following extracts which I have made from the first volume of "The Questions of King Milinda:" —

The King said: "Nagasena, is there any one who after death is not reindividualized?" Nagasena answered: "A sinful being is reindividualized; a sinless one is not." (p. 50.)

"Is there, Nagasena, such a thing as the soul?" "There is no such thing as soul." (pp. 86–89.) [The same statement is repeated in a later chapter (p. 111), with a qualification: "*In the highest sense*, O King, there is no such thing."]

"Is there any being, Nagasena, who transmigrates from this body to another?" "No: there is not." (p. 112.)

NIRVANA

"Where there is no transmigration, Nagasena, can there be rebirth?" "Yes: there can."

"Does he, Nagasena, who is about to be reborn, know that he will be reborn?" "Yes: he knows it, O King." (p. 113.)

Naturally the Western reader may ask, — "How can there be reindividualization without a soul? How can there be rebirth without transmigration? How can there be personal foreknowledge of rebirth without personality?" But the answers to such questions will not be found in the work cited.

It would be wrong to suppose that the citations given offer any exceptional difficulty. As to the doctrine of the annihilation of Self, the testimony of nearly all those Buddhist texts now accessible to English readers is overwhelming. Perhaps the Sutra of the Great Decease furnishes the most remarkable evidence contained in the "Sacred Books of the East." In its account of the Eight Stages of Deliverance leading to Nirvana, it explicitly describes what we should be justified in calling, from our Western point of view, the process of absolute annihilation. We are told that in the first of these eight stages the Buddhist seeker after truth still retains the ideas of form — subjective and objective. In the second stage he loses the subjective idea of form, and views forms as external phenomena only. In the third stage the sense of the approaching perception of larger truth comes to him. In the fourth stage he passes beyond all ideas of form, ideas of resistance, and ideas of distinction; and there remains to him only the idea of infinite space. In the fifth stage the idea of infinite space vanishes, and the thought comes: *It is all infinite reason.* [Here is the uttermost limit, many might suppose, of pantheistic idealism; but it is only the half way resting-place on the path which the Buddhist thinker must pursue.] In the sixth stage the thought comes, "*Nothing at all exists.*" In the seventh stage the idea of nothingness itself vanishes. In the eighth stage all sensations and ideas cease to exist. And *after* this comes Nirvana.

The same sutra, in recounting the death of the Buddha, represents him as rapidly passing through the first, second, third, and fourth stages of meditation to enter into "that state of mind to which the Infinity of Space alone is present," — and thence into "that state of mind to which the Infinity of Thought alone is present," — and thence into "that state of mind to which nothing at all is specially present," — and thence into "that state of mind between consciousness and unconsciousness," — and thence into "that state of mind in which the consciousness both of sensations and of ideas has wholly passed away."

For the reader who has made any serious attempt to obtain a general idea of Buddhism, such citations are scarcely necessary; since the fundamental doctrine of the concatenation of cause and effect contains the same denial of the reality of Self and suggests the same enigmas. Illusion produces action or Karma; Karma, self-consciousness; self-consciousness, individuality; individuality, the senses; the senses, contact; contact, feeling; feeling, desire; desire, union; union, conception; conception, birth; birth, sorrow and decrepitude and death. Doubtless the reader knows the doctrine of the destruction of the twelve Nidanas; and it is needless here to repeat it at length. But he may be reminded of the teaching that by the cessation of contact feeling is destroyed; by that of feeling, individuality; and by that of individuality, *self-consciousness*.

Evidently, without a preliminary solution of the riddles offered by such texts, any effort to learn the meaning of Nirvana is hopeless. Before being able to comprehend the true meaning of those sutras now made familiar to English readers by translation, it is necessary to understand that the common Occidental ideas of God and Soul, of matter, of spirit, have no existence in Buddhist philosophy; their places being occupied by concepts having no real counterparts in Western religious thought. Above all, it is necessary that the reader should expel from his mind the theological idea of Soul. The texts already quoted should have made it clear that in Buddhist philosophy there is no personal transmigration, and no individual permanent Soul.

II

"O Bhagavat, the idea of a self is no idea; and the idea of a being, or a living person, or a person, is no idea. And why? Because the blessed Buddhas are freed from all ideas." — *The Diamond-Cutter*.

And now let us try to understand what it is that dies, and what it is that is reborn, — what it is that commits faults and what it is that suffers penalties, — what passes from states of woe to states of bliss, — what enters into Nirvana after the destruction of self-consciousness, — what survives "extinction" and has power to return out of Nirvana, — what experiences the Four Infinite Feelings after all finite feeling has been annihilated.

It is not the sentient and conscious Self that enters Nirvana. The Ego is only a temporary aggregate of countless illusions, a phantom-shell, a bubble sure to break. It is a creation of Karma, — or rather, as a Buddhist friend insists, it *is* Karma. To comprehend the statement fully, the reader should know that, in this Oriental philosophy, acts and thoughts are forces integrating themselves into material and mental phenomena,

— into what we call objective and subjective appearances. The very earth we tread upon, — the mountains and forests, the rivers and seas, the world and its moon, the visible universe in short, — *is the integration of acts and thoughts*, is Karma, or, at least, Being conditioned by Karma.[1]

---

[1] "The aggregate actions of all sentient beings give birth to the varieties of mountains, rivers, countries, etc. ... Their eyes, nostrils, ears, tongues, bodies, — as well as their gardens, woods, farms, residences, servants, and maids, — men imagine to be their own possessions; but they are, in truth, only results produced by innumerable actions." — Kuroda, *Outlines of the Mahayana*.

"Grass, trees, earth, — all these shall become Buddha." — Chū-in-kyō."

"Even swords and things of metal are manifestations of spirit: within them exist all virtues [*or* '*power*'] in their fullest development and perfection." — Hizō-hō-yaku.

"When called sentient or non-sentient, matter is Law-Body [*or* '*spiritual body*']." — Chishō-hishō.

"The Apparent Doctrine treats of the four great elements [*earth, fire, water, air*] as non-sentient. But in the Hidden Doctrine these are said to be the Sammya-Shin [*Samya-Kaya*], or Body-Accordant of the Nyōrai [Tathâgata]." — Soku-shin-jō-butsu-gi.

"When every phase of our mind shall be in accord with the mind of Buddha, ... then there will not be even one particle of dust that does not enter into Buddhahood." — Engaku-Shō.

The Karma-Ego we call Self is mind and is body; — both perpetually decay; both are perpetually renewed. From the unknown beginning, this double-phenomenon, objective and subjective, has been alternately dissolved and integrated: each integration is a birth; each dissolution a death. There is no other birth or death but the birth and death of Karma in some form or condition. But at each rebirth the reintegration is never the reintegration of the identical phenomenon, but of another to which it gives rise, — as growth begets growth, as motion produces motion. So that the phantom-self changes not only as to form and condition, but as to actual personality with every reëmbodiment. There is one Reality; but there is no permanent individual, no constant personality: there is only phantom-self, and phantom succeeds to phantom, as undulation to undulation, over the ghostly Sea of Birth and Death. And even as the storming of a sea is a motion of undulation, not of translation, — even as it is the form of the wave only, not the wave itself, that travels, — so in the passing of lives there is only the rising and the vanishing of forms, — forms mental, forms material. The fathomless Reality does not pass. "All forms," it is written in the *Kongō-hannya-haramitsu-Kyō*,[1] "are unreal: he who rises above all forms is the Buddha." But what can remain to rise above all forms after the total disintegration of body and the final dissolution of mind?

Unconsciously dwelling behind the false consciousness of imperfect man, — beyond sensation, perception, thought, — wrapped in the envelope of what we call soul (which in truth is only a thickly woven veil of illusion), is the eternal and divine, the Absolute Reality: not a soul, not a personality, but the All-Self without selfishness, — the *Muga no Taiga*, — the Buddha enwombed in Karma. Within every phantom-self dwells this divine: yet the innumerable are but one. Within every creature incarnate sleeps the Infinite Intelligence unevolved, hidden, unfelt, unknown, — yet destined from all the eternities to waken at last, to rend away the ghostly web of sensuous mind, to break forever its chrysalis of flesh, and pass to the supreme

[1] *Vagra-pragñâ-pâramita-Sutra.*

NIRVANA

conquest of Space and Time. Wherefore it is written in the *Kegon-Kyō* (Avatamsaka-Sutra): "Child of Buddha, there is not even one living being that has not the wisdom of the Tathâgata. It is only because of their vain thoughts and affections that all beings are not conscious of this. . . . I will teach them the holy Way; — I will make them forsake their foolish thoughts, and cause them to see that the vast and deep intelligence which dwells within them is not different from the wisdom of the very Buddha."

Here we may pause to consider the correspondence between these fundamental Buddhist theories and the concepts of Western science. It will be evident that the Buddhist denial of the reality of the apparitional world is not a denial of the reality of phenomena as phenomena, nor a denial of the forces producing phenomena objectively or subjectively. For the negation of Karma as Karma would involve the negation of the entire Buddhist system. The true declaration is, that what we perceive is never reality in itself, and that even the Ego that perceives is an unstable plexus of aggregates of feelings which are themselves unstable and in the nature of illusions. This position is scientifically strong, — perhaps impregnable. Of substance in itself we certainly know nothing: we are conscious of the universe as a vast play of forces only; and, even while we discern the general relative meaning of laws expressed in the action of those forces, all that which is Non-Ego is revealed to us merely through the vibrations of a nervous structure never exactly the same in any two human beings. Yet through such varying and imperfect perception we are sufficiently assured of the impermanency of all forms, — of all aggregates objective or subjective.

The test of reality is persistence; and the Buddhist, finding in the visible universe only a perpetual flux of phenomena, declares the material aggregate unreal because non-persistent, — unreal, at least, as a bubble, a cloud, or a mirage. Again, relation is the universal form of thought; but since relation is impermanent, how can thought be persistent? . . . Judged from these points of view, Buddhist doctrine is not Anti-Realism, but a veritable

Transfigured Realism, finding just expression in the exact words of Herbert Spencer:—
"Every feeling and thought being but transitory;—an entire life made up of such feelings and thoughts being also but transitory;—nay, the objects amid which life is passed, though less transitory, being severally in the course of losing their individualities, whether quickly or slowly,—*we learn that the one thing permanent is the Unknowable Reality hidden under all these changing shapes.*"

Likewise, the teaching of Buddhism, that what we call Self is an impermanent aggregate,—a sensuous illusion,—will prove, if patiently analyzed, scarcely possible for any serious thinker to deny. Mind, as known to the scientific psychologist, is composed of feelings and the relations between feelings; and feelings are composed of units of simple sensation which are physiologically coincident with minute nervous shocks. All the sense-organs are fundamentally alike, being evolutional modifications of the same morphological elements;—and all the senses are modifications of touch. Or, to use the simplest possible language, the organs of sense — sight, smell, taste, even hearing — have been alike developed from the skin! Even the human brain itself, by the modern testimony of histology and embryology, "is, at its first beginning, merely an infolding of the epidermic layer;" and thought, physiologically and evolutionally, is thus a modification of touch. Certain vibrations, acting through the visual apparatus, cause within the brain those motions which are followed by the sensations of light and color; — other vibrations, acting upon the auditory mechanism, give rise to the sensation of sound; — other vibrations, setting up changes in specialized tissue, produce sensations of taste, smell, touch. All our knowledge is derived and developed, directly or indirectly, from physical sensation, — from touch. Of course this is no ultimate explanation, because nobody can tell us *what feels the touch*. "Everything physical," well said Schopenhauer, "is at the same time metaphysical." But science fully justifies the Buddhist position that what we call Self is a bundle of sensations, emotions, sentiments, ideas, memories, all relating to the *physical* experiences of the race and the individual, and that our wish for immortality is a wish for the eternity of this merely sensuous and selfish consciousness. And science even supports the Buddhist denial of the permanence of the sensuous Ego. "Psychology," says Wundt, "proves that not only our sense-perceptions, but the memorial images that renew them, depend for their origin upon the functionings of the organs of sense and movement. . . . A continuance of this sensuous consciousness must appear to her irreconcilable with the facts of her experience. And surely we may well doubt whether such continuance is an ethical requisite: more, whether the fulfillment of the wish for it, if possible, were not an intolerable destiny."

III

"O Subhûti, if I had had an idea of a being, of a living being, or of a person, I should also have had an idea of malevolence. . . . A gift should not be given by any one who believes in form, sound, smell, taste, or anything that can be touched." — *The Diamond-Cutter.*

The doctrine of the impermanency of the conscious Ego is not only the most remarkable in Buddhist philosophy: it is also, morally, one of the most important. Perhaps the ethical value of this teaching has never yet been fairly estimated by any Western thinker. How much of human unhappiness has been caused, directly and indirectly, by opposite beliefs, — by the delusion of stability, — by the delusion that distinctions of character, condition, class, creed, are settled by immutable law, — and the delusion of a changeless, immortal, sentient soul, destined, by divine caprice, to eternities of bliss or eternities of fire! Doubtless the ideas of a deity moved by everlasting hate, — of soul as a permanent, changeless entity destined to changeless states, — of sin as unatonable and of penalty as never-ending, — were not without value in former savage stages of social development. But in the course of our future evolution they must be utterly got rid of; and it may be hoped that the contact of Western with Oriental thought will have for one happy result the acceleration of their decay. While even the feelings which they have developed linger with us, there can be no true spirit of tolerance, no sense of human brotherhood, no wakening of universal love.

Buddhism, on the other hand, recognizing no permanency, no finite stabilities, no distinctions of character or class or race, except as passing phenomena, — nay, no difference even between gods and men, — has been essentially the religion of tolerance. Demon and angel are but varying manifestations of the same Karma; — hell and heaven mere temporary halting-places upon the journey to eternal peace. For all beings there is but one law, — immutable and divine: the law by which the lowest *must* rise to the place of the highest, — the law by which the worst *must* become the best, — the law by which the vilest *must* become a Buddha. In such a system there is no room for prejudice and for hatred. Ignorance alone is the source of wrong and pain; and all ignorance must finally be dissipated in infinite light *through the decomposition of Self*.

Certainly while we still try to cling to the old theories of permanent personality, and of a single incarnation only for each individual, we can find no moral meaning in the universe as it exists. Modern knowledge can discover no justice in the cosmic process; — the very most it can offer us by way of ethical encouragement is that the unknowable forces are not forces of pure malevolence. "Neither moral nor immoral," to quote Huxley, "but simply unmoral." Evolutional science cannot be made to accord with the notion of indissoluble personality; and if we accept its teaching of mental growth and inheritance, we must also accept its teaching of individual dissolution and of the cosmos as inexplicable. It assures us, indeed, that the higher faculties of man have been developed through struggle and pain, and will long continue to be so developed; but it also assures us that evolution is inevitably followed by dissolution, — that the highest point of development is the point likewise from which retrogression begins. And if we are each and all mere perishable forms of being, — doomed to pass away like plants and trees, — what consolation can we find in the assurance that we are suffering for the benefit of the future? How can it concern us whether humanity become more or less happy in another myriad ages, if there remains nothing for us but to live and die in comparative misery? Or, to repeat the irony of Huxley, "what compensation does the Eohippus get for his sorrows in the fact that, some millions of years afterwards, one of his descendants wins the Derby?"

But the cosmic process may assume quite another aspect if we can persuade ourselves, like the Buddhist, that all being is Unity, — that personality is but a delusion hiding reality, — that all distinctions of "I" and "thou" are ghostly films spun out of perishable sensation, — that even Time and Place as revealed to our petty senses are phantasms, — that the past and the present and the future are veritably One. Suppose the winner of the Derby quite well able to remember having been the Eohippus? Suppose the being, once man, able to look back through all veils of death and birth, through all evolutions of evolution, even to the moment of the first faint growth of sentiency out of non-sentiency; — able to remember, like the Buddha of the Jatakas, all the experiences of his myriad incarnations, and to relate them like fairy-tales for the sake of another Ananda?

We have seen that it is not the Self but the Non-Self — the one reality underlying all phenomena — which passes from form to form. The striving for Nirvana is a struggle perpetual between false and true, light and darkness, the sensual and the supersensual; and the ultimate victory can be gained only by the total decomposition of the mental and the physical individuality. Not one conquest of self can suffice: millions of selves must be overcome. For the false Ego is a compound of countless ages, — possesses a vitality enduring beyond universes. At each breaking and shedding of the chrysalis a new chrysalis appears, — more tenous, perhaps, more diaphanous, but woven of like sensuous material, — a mental and physical texture spun by Karma from the inherited illusions, passions, desires, pains and pleasures, of innumerable lives. But what is it that feels? — the phantom or the reality?

All phenomena of *Self*-consciousness belong to the false self, — but only as a physiologist might say that sensation is a product of the sensiferous apparatus, which would not explain sensation. No more in Buddhism than in physiological psychology is there any real teaching of *two* feeling entities. In Buddhism the only entity is the Absolute; and to that entity the false self stands in the relation of a medium through which right perception is deflected and distorted, — in which and because of which sentiency and impulse become possible. The unconditioned Absolute is above all relations : it has nothing of what we call pain or pleasure ; it knows no difference of " I " and " thou," — no distinction of place or time. But while conditioned by the illusion of personality, it is aware of pain or pleasure, as a dreamer perceives unrealities without being conscious of their unreality. Pleasures and pains and all the feelings relating to self-consciousness are hallucinations. The false self exists only as a state of sleep exists ; and sentiency and desire, and all the sorrows and passions of being, exist only as illusions of that sleep.

But here we reach a point at which science and Buddhism diverge. Modern psychology recognizes no feelings not evolutionally developed through the experiences of the race and the individual ; but Buddhism asserts the existence of feelings which are immorta' and divine. It declares that in this Karma-state the greater part of our sensations, perceptions, ideas, thoughts, are related only to the phantom self; — that our mental life is little more than a flow of feelings and desires belonging to selfishness; — that our loves and hates, and hopes and fears, and pleasures and pains, are illusions;[1] — but it also declares there are higher feelings, more or less latent within us, according to our degree of knowledge, which have nothing to do with the false self, and which are eternal.

Though science pronounces the ultimate nature of pleasures and pains to be inscrutable, it partly confirms the Buddhist teaching of their impermanent character. Both appear to belong rather to secondary than to primary elements of feeling, and both to be evolutions, — forms of sensation developed, through billions of life-experiences, out of primal conditions in which there can have been neither real pleasure nor real pain, but only the vaguest dull sentiency. The higher the evolution the more pain, and the larger the vol-

[1] "Pleasures and pains have their origin from touch: where there is no touch, they do not arise." — *Atthakavagga*, 11.

NIRVANA 235

time of all sensation. After the state of equilibration has been reached, the volume of feeling will begin to diminish. The finer pleasures and the keener pains must first become extinct; then by gradual stages the less complex feelings, according to their complexity; till at last, in all the refrigerating planet, there will survive not even the simplest sensation possible to the lowest form of life.

But, according to the Buddhist, the highest moral feelings survive races and suns and universes. The purely unselfish feelings, impossible to grosser natures, belong to the Absolute. In generous natures the divine becomes sentient, — quickens within the shell of illusion, as a child quickens in the womb (whence illusion itself is called The Womb of the Tathâgata). In yet higher natures the feelings which are not of self find room for powerful manifestation, — shine through the phantom-Ego as light through a vase. Such are purely unselfish love, larger than individual being, — supreme compassion, — perfect benevolence: they are not of man, but of the Buddha within the man. And as these expand, all the feelings of self begin to thin and weaken. The condition of the phantom-Ego simultaneously purifies: all those opacities which darkened the reality of Mind within the mirage of mind begin to illumine; and the sense of the infinite, like a thrilling of light, passes through the dream of personality into the awakening divine.[1]

But in the case of the average seeker after truth, this refinement and ultimate decomposition of self can be effected only with lentor inexpressible. The phantom-individuality, though enduring only for the space of a single lifetime, shapes out of the sum of its innate qualities, and out of the sum of its own particular acts and thoughts, the new combination which succeeds it, — a fresh individuality, — another prison of illusion for the Self-without-selfishness.[2] As name and form, the false self dissolves; but its impulses live on and recom-

---

[1] "To reach the state of the perfect and everlasting happiness is the highest Nirvana; for then all mental phenomena — such as desires, etc. — are annihilated. And as such mental phenomena are annihilated, there appears the true nature of true mind with all its innumerable functions and miraculous actions." — KURODA, *Outlines of the Mahâyâna.*

[2] It is on the subject of this propagation and perpetuation of characters that the doctrine of Karma is in partial agree-

bine; and the final destruction of those impulses — the total extinction of their ghostly vitality, — may require a protraction of effort through billions of centuries. Perpetually from the ashes of burnt-out passions subtler passions are born, — perpetually from the graves of illusions new illusions arise. The most powerful of human passions is the last to yield: it persists far into superhuman conditions. Even when its grosser forms have passed away, its tendencies still lurk in those feelings originally derived from it or interwoven with it, — the sensation of beauty, for example, and the delight of the mind in graceful things. On earth these are classed among the higher feelings. But in a supramundane state their indulgence is fraught with peril: a touch or a look may cause the broken fetters of sensual bondage to reform. Beyond all worlds of sex there are strange zones in which thoughts and memories become tangible and visible objective facts, — in which emotional fancies are materialized,— in which the least unworthy wish may prove creative.

ment with the modern scientific teaching of the hereditary transmission of tendencies.

It may be said, in Western religious phraseology, that throughout the greater part of this vast pilgrimage, and in all the zones of desire, the temptations increase according to the spiritual strength of resistance. With every successive ascent there is a further expansion of the possibilities of enjoyment, an augmentation of power, a heightening of sensation. Immense the reward of self-conquest; but whosoever strives for that reward strives after emptiness. One must not desire heaven as a state of pleasure; it has been written, *Erroneous thoughts as to the joys of heaven are still entwined by the fast cords of lust.* One must not wish to become a god or an angel. "Whatsoever brother, O Bhikkus," — the Teacher said, — "may have adopted the religious life thinking, to himself, '*By this morality I shall become an angel*,' his mind does not incline to zeal, perseverance, exertion." Perhaps the most vivid exposition of the duty of the winner of happiness is that given in the Sutra of the Great King of Glory. This great king, coming into possession of all imaginable wealth and power, abstains from enjoyments, despises splendors, refuses the caresses of a Queen dowered with "the beauty of the gods," and bids her demand of him, out of her own lips, that he forsake her. She, with dutiful sweetness, but not without natural tears, obeys him; and he passes at once out of existence. Every such refusal of the prizes gained by virtue helps to cause a still more fortunate birth in a still loftier state of being. But no state should be desired; and it is only after the wish for Nirvana itself has ceased that Nirvana can be attained.

And now we may venture for a little while into the most fantastic region of Buddhist ontology, — since, without some definite notion of the course of psychical evolution therein described, the suggestive worth of the system cannot be fairly judged. Certainly I am asking the reader to consider a theory about what is beyond the uttermost limit of possible human knowledge. But as much of the Buddhist doctrine as can be studied and tested within the limit of human knowledge is found to accord with scientific opinion better than does any other religious hypothesis; and some of the Buddhist teachings prove to be incomprehensible anticipations of modern scientific discovery, — can it, therefore, seem unreasonable to claim that even the pure fancies of a faith so much older than our own, and so much more capable of being reconciled with the widest expansions of nineteenth-century thought, deserve at least respectful consideration?

IV

"Non-existence is only the entrance to the Great Vehicle." — *Daibon-Kyōi.*

"And in which way is it, Siha, that one speaking truly could say of me: 'The Samana Gotama maintains annihilation; — he teaches the doctrine of annihilation'? I proclaim, Siha, the annihilation of lust, of ill-will, of delusion; I proclaim the annihilation of the manifold conditions (of heart) which are evil and not good." — *Mahavagga,* vi. 31. 7.

"*Nin mité, hō toké*" (see first the person, then preach the law) is a Japanese proverb signifying that Buddhism should be taught according to the capacity of the pupil. And the great systems of Buddhist doctrine are actually divided into progressive stages (five usually), to be studied in succession, or otherwise, according to the intellectual ability of

NIRVANA

the learner. Also there are many varieties of special doctrine held by the different sects and sub-sects, — so that, to make any satisfactory outline of Buddhist ontology, it is necessary to shape a synthesis of the more important and non-conflicting among these many tenets. I need scarcely say that popular Buddhism does not include concepts such as we have been examining. The people hold to the simpler creed of a veritable transmigration of souls. The people understand Karma only as the law that makes the punishment or reward of faults committed in previous lives. The people do not trouble themselves about *Nehan* or Nirvana;[1] but they think much about heaven (*Gokuraku*), which the members of many sects believe can be attained immediately after this life by the spirits of the good. The

---

[1] Scarcely a day passes that I do not hear such words uttered as ingwa, gokuraku, gōshō, — or other words referring to Karma, heaven, future life, past life, etc. But I have never heard a man or woman of the people use the word "Nehan;" and whenever I have ventured to question such about Nirvana, I found that its philosophical meaning was unknown. On the other hand, the Japanese scholar speaks of Nehan as the reality, — of heaven, either as a temporary condition or as a parable.

followers of the greatest and richest of the modern sects — the *Shinshū* — hold that, by the invocation of Amida, a righteous person can pass at once after death to the great Paradise of the West, — the Paradise of the Lotos-Flower-Birth. I am taking no account of popular beliefs in this little study, nor of doctrines peculiar to any one sect only.

But there are many differences in the higher teaching as to the attainment of Nirvana. Some authorities hold that the supreme happiness can be won, or at least seen, even on this earth; while others declare that the present world is too corrupt to allow of a perfect life, and that only by winning, through good deeds, the privilege of rebirth into a better world, can men hope for opportunity to practice that holiness which leads to the highest bliss. The latter opinion, which posits the superior conditions of being in other worlds, better expresses the general thought of contemporary Buddhism in Japan.

The conditions of human and of animal being belong to what are termed the Worlds of Desire (*Yoku-Kai*), — which are four in number. Below these are the states of torment or hells (*Jigoku*), about which many curious things are written; but neither the Yoku-Kai nor the Jigoku need be considered in relation to the purpose of this little essay. We have only to do with the course of spiritual progress from the world of men up to Nirvana, — assuming, with modern Buddhism, that the pilgrimage through death and birth must continue, for the majority of mankind at least, even after the attainment of the highest conditions possible upon this globe. The way rises from terrestrial conditions to other and superior worlds, — passing first through the Six Heavens of Desire (*Yoku-Ten*); — thence through the Seventeen Heavens of Form (*Shiki-Kai*); — and lastly through the Four Heavens of Formlessness (*Mushiki-Kai*), beyond which lies Nirvana.

The requirements of physical life — the need of food, rest, and sexual relations — continue to be felt in the Heavens of Desire, — which would seem to be higher physical worlds rather than what we commonly understand by the expression "heavens." Indeed, the conditions in some of them are such as might be supposed to exist in planets more favored than our own, — in larger spheres warmed by a more genial sun. And some Buddhist texts actually place them in remote constellations, — declaring that the Path leads from star to star, from galaxy to galaxy, from universe to universe, up to the Limit of Existence.[1]

In the first of the heavens of this zone, called the Heaven of the Four Kings (*Shi-Tennō-Ten*), life lasts five times longer than life on this earth according to number of years, and each year there is equal to fifty terrestrial years. But its inhabitants eat and drink, and marry and give in marriage, much after the fashion of mankind. In the succeeding heaven (*Sanjiu-san-Ten*), the duration of life is doubled, while all other conditions are correspondingly improved; and the grosser forms

---

[1] This astronomical localization of higher conditions of being, or of other "Buddha-fields," may provoke a smile; but it suggests undeniable possibilities. There is no absurdity in supposing that potentialities of life and growth and development really pass, with nebular diffusion and concentration, from expired systems to new systems. Indeed, not to suppose this, in our present state of knowledge, is scarcely possible for the rational mind.

of passion disappear. The union of the sexes persists, but in a manner curiously similar to that which a certain Father of the Christian Church wished might become possible, — a simple embrace producing a new being. In the third heaven (called *Emma-Ten*), where longevity is again doubled, the slightest touch may create life. In the fourth, or Heaven of Contentment (*Tochita-Ten*), longevity is further increased. In the fifth, or Heaven of the Transmutation of Pleasure (*Keraku-Ten*), strange new powers are gained. Subjective pleasures become changed at will into objective pleasures; — thoughts as well as wishes become creative forces; — and even the act of seeing may cause conception and birth. In the sixth heaven (*Také-jizai-Ten*), the powers obtained in the fifth heaven are further developed; and the subjective pleasures transmuted into objective can be presented to others, or shared with others, — like material gifts. But the look of an instant, — one glance of the eye, — may generate a new Karma.

The Yoku-Kai are all heavens of sensuous life, — heavens such as might answer to the dreams of artists and lovers and poets. But those who are able to traverse them without falling — (and a fall, be it observed, is not difficult) — pass into the Supersensual Zone, first entering the Heavens of Luminous Observation of Existence and of Calm Meditation upon Existence (*Ujin-ushi-shōryo*, or *Kakkwan*). These are in number three, — each higher than the preceding, — and are named The Heaven of Sanctity, The Heaven of Higher Sanctity, and The Heaven of Great Sanctity. After these come the heavens called the Heavens of Luminous Observation of Non-Existence and of Calm Meditation upon Non-Existence (*Mūjin-mushi-shōryo*). These also are three; and the names of them in their order signify, Lesser Light, Light Unfathomable, and Light Making Sound, or, Light-Sonorous. Here there is attained the highest degree of supersensuous joy possible to temporary conditions. Above are the states named *Riki-shōryo*, or the Heavens of the Meditation of the Abandonment of Joy. The names of these states in their ascending order are, Lesser Purity, Purity Unfathomable, and Purity Supreme. In them neither joy nor pain, nor forceful feeling of any sort exist: there is a mild negative pleasure only, — the pleasure of heavenly Equanimity.[1] Higher than these heavens are the eight spheres of Calm Meditation upon the Abandonment of all Joy and Pleasure (*Riki-raku-shōryo*). They are called The Cloudless, Holiness-Manifest, Vast Results, Empty of Name, Void of Heat, Fair-Appearing, Vision-Perfecting, and The Limit of Form. Herein pleasure and pain, and name and form, pass utterly away. But there remain ideas and thoughts.

He who can pass through these supersensual realms enters at once into the *Mushiki-Kai*, — the spheres of Formlessness. These are four. In the first state of the Mushiki-Kai, all sense of individuality is lost: even the thought of name and form becomes extinct, and there survives only the idea of Infinite Space, or Emptiness. In the second

[1] One is reminded by this conception of Mr. Spencer's beautiful definition of Equanimity: — "Equanimity may be compared to white light, which, though composed of numerous colors, is colorless; while pleasurable and painful moods of mind may be compared to the modifications of light that result from increasing the proportions of some rays, and decreasing the proportions of others." — *Principles of Psychology*.

state of the Mushiki-Kai, this idea of space vanishes; and its place is filled by the Idea of Infinite Reason. But this idea of reason is anthropomorphic: it is an illusion; and it fades out in the third state of the Mushiki-Kai, which is called the "State-of-Nothing-to-take-hold-of," or *Mū-sho-ū-shō-jō*. Here is only the Idea of Infinite Nothingness. But even this condition has been reached by the aid of the action of the personal mind. This action ceases: then the fourth state of the Mushiki-Kai is reached, — the *Hisō-hihisō-shō*, or the state of "neither-namelessness-nor-not-namelessness." Something of personal mentality continues to float vaguely here, — the very uttermost expiring vibration of Karma, — the last vanishing haze of being. It melts; — and the immeasurable revelation comes. The dreaming Buddha, freed from the last ghostly bond of Self, rises at once into the "infinite bliss" of Nirvana.[1]

But every being does not pass through all the states above enumerated: the power to

---

[1] The expression "infinite bliss" as synonymous with Nirvana is taken from the *Questions of King Milinda*.

rise swiftly or slowly depends upon the acquisition of merit as well as upon the character of the Karma to be overcome. Some beings pass to Nirvana immediately after the present life; some after a single new birth; some after two or three births; while many rise directly from this world into one of the Supersensuous Heavens. All such are called *Chō*, — the Leapers, — of whom the highest class reach Nirvana at once after their death as men or women. There are two great divisions of Chō, — the *Fu-Kwan*, or Never-Returning-Ones,[1] and the *Kwan*, Returning Ones, or *revenants*. Sometimes the return may be in the nature of a prolonged retrogression; and, according to a Buddhist legend of the origin of the world, the first men were beings who had fallen from the *Kwō-on-Ten*, or Heaven of Sonorous Light. A remarkable fact about the whole theory of progression is that the progression is not conceived of

[1] In the Sutra of the Great Decease we find the instance of a woman reaching this condition: — "The Sister Nanda, O Ananda, by the destruction of the five bonds that bind people to this world, has become an inhabitant of the highest heaven, — there to pass entirely away, — thence never to return."

(except in very rare cases) as an advance in straight lines, but as an advance by undulations, — a psychical rhythm of motion. This is exemplified by the curious Buddhist classification of the different short courses by which the Kwan or *revenants* may hope to reach Nirvana. These short courses are divided into Even and Uneven; — the former includes an equal number of heavenly and of earthly rebirths; while in the latter class the heavenly and the earthly intermediate rebirths are not equal in number. There are four kinds of these intermediate stages. A Japanese friend has drawn for me the accompanying diagrams, which explain the subject clearly.

Fantastic this may be called; but it harmonizes with the truth that all progress is necessarily rhythmical.

Though all beings do not pass through every stage of the great journey, all beings who attain to the highest enlightenment, by any course whatever, acquire certain faculties not belonging to particular conditions of birth, but only to particular conditions of psychical development. These are, the *Roku-Jindzū*

NIRVANA REACHED FROM THE HEAVENS THROUGH 3 EVEN BIRTHS:—

— THROUGH 3 UNEVEN BIRTHS:—

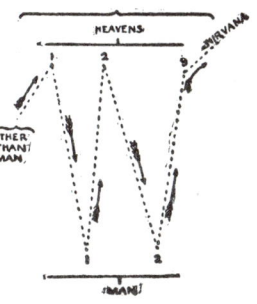

NIRVANA REACHED FROM THE STATE OF MAN THROUGH 3 EVEN BIRTHS:—

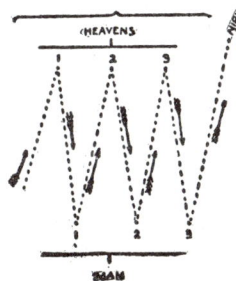

— THROUGH 3 UNEVEN BIRTHS:—

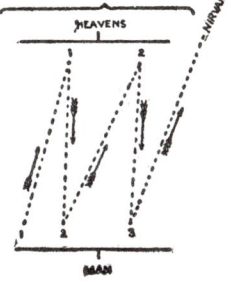

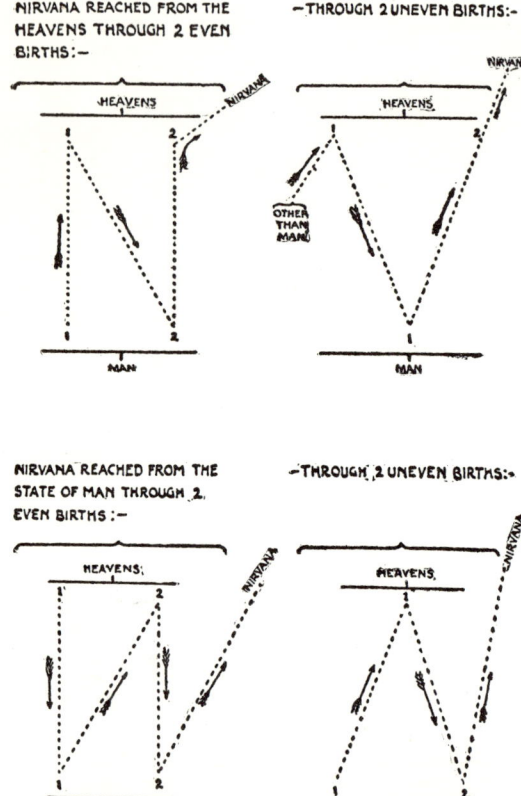

(Abhidjñâ), or Six Supernatural Powers:[1] —
(1) *Shin-Kyō-Tsu*, the power of passing anywhither through any obstacles, — through solid walls, for example; — (2) *Tengen-Tsū*, the power of infinite vision; — (3) *Tenni-Tsū*, the power of infinite hearing; — (4) *Tashin - Tsū*, the power of knowing the thoughts of all other beings; — (5) *Shuku-jū-Tsū*, the power of remembering former births; — (6) *Rojin - Tsū*, infinite wisdom with the power of entering at will into Nirvana. The Roku-jindzū first begin to develop in the state of *Shōmon* (Sravaka), and expand in the higher conditions of *Engaku* (Pratyeka-Buddha) and of Bosatsu (Bodhisattva or Mahâsattva). The powers of the Shōmon may be exerted over two thousand worlds; those of the Engaku or Bosatsu, over three thousand; — but the powers of Buddhahood extend over the total cosmos. In the

[1] Different Buddhist systems give different enumerations of these mysterious powers whereof the Chinese names literally signify: — (1) Calm - Meditation-outward-pouring-no-obstacle-wisdom; — (2) Heaven-Eye-no-obstacle-wisdom; — (3) Heaven-Ear-no-obstacle-wisdom; — (4) Other-minds-no-obstacle-wisdom; — (5) Former-States-no-obstacle-wisdom; — (6) Leak-Extinction-no-obstacle-wisdom.

first state of holiness, for example, comes the memory of a certain number of former births, together with the capacity to foresee a corresponding number of future births; — in the next higher state the number of births remembered increases; — and in the state of Bosatsu all former births are visible to memory. But the Buddha sees not only all of his own former births, but likewise all births that ever have been or can be, — and all the thoughts and acts, past, present, or future, of all past, present, or future beings. . . . Now these dreams of supernatural power merit attention because of the ethical teaching in regard to them, — the same which is woven through every Buddhist hypothesis, rational or unthinkable, — the teaching of self-abnegation. The Supernatural Powers must never be used for personal pleasure, but only for the highest beneficence, — the propagation of doctrine, the saving of men. Any exercise of them for lesser ends might result in their loss, — would certainly signify retrogression in the path.[1]

---

[1] Beings who have reached the state of Engaku or of Bosatsu are not supposed capable of retrogression, or of any serious error; but it is otherwise in lower spiritual states.

To show them for the purpose of exciting admiration or wonder were to juggle wickedly with what is divine; and the Teacher himself is recorded to have once severely rebuked a needless display of them by a disciple.[1]

This giving up not only of one life, but of countless lives, — not only of one world, but of innumerable worlds, — not only of natural but also of supernatural pleasures, — not only of selfhood but of godhood, — is certainly not for the miserable privilege of ceasing to be, but for a privilege infinitely outweighing all that even paradise can give. Nirvana is no cessation, but an emancipation. It means only the passing of conditioned being into unconditioned being, — the fading of all mental and physical phantoms into the light of Formless Omnipotence and Omniscience. But the Buddhist hypothesis holds some suggestion of the persistence of that which has once been able to remember all births and states of limited being, — the persistence of the identity of the Buddhas even

[1] See a curious legend in the Vinaya texts, — *Kullavagga*, v. 8, 2.

in Nirvana, notwithstanding the teaching that all Buddhas are one. How reconcile this doctrine of monism with the assurance of various texts that the being who enters Nirvana can, when so desirous, reassume an earthly personality? There are some very remarkable texts on this subject in the Sutra of the Lotos of the Good Law: those for instance in which the Tathâgata Prabhûtarâtna is pictured as sitting "*perfectly extinct upon his throne*," and speaking before a vast assembly to which he has been introduced as "the great Seer who, *although perfectly extinct for many kôtis of œons*, now comes to hear the Law." These texts themselves offer us the riddle of multiplicity in unity; for the Tathâgata Prabhûtarâtna and the myriads of other extinct Buddhas who appear simultaneously, are said to have been all incarnations of but a single Buddha.

A reconciliation is offered by the hypothesis of what might be called a *pluristic monism*, — a sole reality composed of groups of consciousness, at once independent and yet interdependent, — or, to speak of pure mind in terms of matter, *an atomic spiritual ultimate*. This

NIRVANA

hypothesis, though not doctrinably enunciated in Buddhist texts, is distinctly implied both by text and commentary. The Absolute of Buddhism is one as ether is one. Ether is conceivable only as a composition of units.[1]

[1] This position, it will be observed, is very dissimilar from that of Hartmann, who holds that "all plurality of individuation belongs to the sphere of phenomenality." (vol. ii. page 233 of English translation.) One is rather reminded of the thought of Galton that human beings "may contribute more or less unconsciously to the manifestation of a far higher life than our own, — somewhat as the individual cells of one of the more complex animals contribute to the manifestation of its higher order of personality." (*Hereditary Genius*, p. 361.) Another thought of Galton's, expressed on the same page of the work just quoted from, is still more strongly suggestive of the Buddhist concept: — "We must not permit ourselves to consider each human or other personality as something supernaturally added to the stock of nature, but rather as a segregation of what already existed, under a new shape, and as a regular consequence of previous conditions. . . . Neither must we be misled by the word 'individuality.' . . . We may look upon each individual as something not wholly detached from its parent-source, — as a wave that has been lifted and shaped by normal conditions in an unknown and illimitable ocean."

The reader should remember that the Buddhist hypothesis does not imply either individuality or personality in Nirvana, but simple entity, — not a spiritual *body*, in our meaning of the term, but only a divine consciousness. "Heart," in the

The Absolute is conceivable only (according to any attempt at a synthesis of the Japanese doctrines) as composed of Buddhas. But here the student finds himself voyaging farther, perhaps, beyond the bar of the thinkable than Western philosophers have ever ventured. All are One; — each by union becomes equal with All! We are not only bidden to imagine the ultimate reality as composed of units of conscious being, — but to believe each unit

sense of divine mind, is a term used in some Japanese texts to describe such entity. In the *Dai-Nichi Kyō Sō* (Commentary on the Dai-Nichi Sutra), for example, is the statement: — "When all seeds of Karma-life are entirely burnt out and annihilated, then the *vacuum-pure* Bodhi-heart is reached." (I may observe that Buddhist metaphysicians use the term "vacuum-bodies" to describe one of the high conditions of entity.) The following, from the fifty-first volume of the work called *Daizō-hō-sū* will also be found interesting: — "By experience the Tathâgata possesses all forms, — forms for multitude numberless as the dust-grains of the universe. . . . The Tathâgata gets himself born in such places as he desires, or in accord with the desire of others, and there saves [lit., 'carries over' — that is, over the Sea of Birth and Death] all sentient beings. Wheresoever his will finds an abiding-point, there is he embodied: this is called Will-Birth Body. . . . The Buddha makes Law his body, and remains pure as empty space: this is called Law-Body."

permanently equal to every other *and infinite in potentiality*.[1] The central reality of every living creature is a pure Buddha: the visible form and thinking self, which encell it, being but Karma. With some degree of truth it might be said that Buddhism substitutes for our theory of a universe of physical atoms the hypothesis of a universe of psychical units. Not that it necessarily denies our theory of physical atoms, but that it assumes a position which might be thus expressed in words: "What you call atoms are really combinations, unstable aggregates, essentially impermanent, and therefore essentially unreal. Atoms are but Karma." And this position is suggestive. We know nothing whatever of the ultimate nature of substance and motion: but we have scientific evidence that the known has been evolved from the unknown; that the atoms of our elements *are* combinations; and that what we call matter and force are but different manifestations of a single and infinite Unknown Reality.

---

[1] Half of this Buddhist thought is really embodied in Tennyson's line, —

"Boundless inward, in the atom; boundless outward, in the Whole."

There are wonderful Buddhist pictures which at first sight appear to have been made, like other Japanese pictures, with bold free sweeps of a skilled brush, but which, when closely examined, prove to have been executed in a much more marvelous manner. The figures, the features, the robes, the aureoles, — also the scenery, the colors, the effects of mist or cloud, — all, even to the tiniest detail of tone or line, have been produced by groupings of microscopic Chinese characters, — tinted according to position, and more or less thickly massed according to need of light or shade. In brief, these pictures are composed entirely out of texts of Sutras: they are mosaics of minute ideographs, — each ideograph a combination of strokes, and the symbol at once of a sound and of an idea.

Is our universe so composed? — an endless phantasmagory made only by combinations of combinations of combinations of combinations of units finding quality and form through unimaginable affinities; — now thickly massed in solid glooms; now palpitating in tremulosities of light and color; always and everywhere grouped by some stupendous art into one vast mosaic of polarities; — yet each unit in itself a complexity inconceivable, and each in itself also a symbol only, a character, a single ideograph of the undecipherable text of the Infinite Riddle? . . . Ask the chemists and the mathematicians.

V

> . . . "All beings that have life shall lay
> Aside their complex form, — that aggregation
> Of *mental* and material qualities
> That gives them, or in heaven or on earth.
> Their fleeting individuality."
> *The Book of the Great Decease.*

In every teleological system there are conceptions which cannot bear the test of modern psychological analysis, and in the foregoing unfilled outline of a great religious hypothesis there will doubtless be recognized some "ghosts of beliefs haunting those mazes of verbal propositions in which metaphysicians habitually lose themselves." But truths will be perceived also, — grand recognitions of the law of ethical evolution, of the price of progress, and of our relation to the changeless Reality abiding beyond all change.

The Buddhist estimate of the enormity of that opposition to moral progress which humanity must overcome is fully sustained by our scientific knowledge of the past and perception of the future. Mental and moral advance has thus far been effected only through constant struggle against inheritances older than reason or moral feeling, — against the instincts and the appetites of primitive brute life. And the Buddhist teaching, that the average man can hope to leave his worse nature behind him only after the lapse of millions of future lives, is much more of a truth than of a theory. Only through millions of births have we been able to reach even this our present imperfect state; and the dark bequests of our darkest past are still strong enough betimes to prevail over reason and ethical feeling. Every future forward pace upon the moral path will have to be taken against the massed effort of millions of ghostly wills. For those past selves which priest and poet have told us to use as steps to higher things are not dead, nor even likely to die for a thousand generations to come: they are too much alive; — they have still power to clutch the climbing feet, — sometimes even to fling back the climber into the primeval slime.

Again, in its legend of the Heavens of Desire, — progress through which depends upon the ability of triumphant virtue to refuse what it has won, — Buddhism gives us a wonder-story full of evolutional truth. The difficulties of moral self-elevation do not disappear with the amelioration of material social conditions ; — in our own day they rather increase. As life becomes more complex, more multiform, so likewise do the obstacles to ethical advance, — so likewise do the results of thoughts and acts. The expansion of intellectual power, the refinement of sensibility, the enlargement of the sympathies, the intensive quickening of the sense of beauty, — all multiply ethical dangers just as certainly as they multiply ethical opportunities. The highest material results of civilization, and the increase of possibilities of pleasure, exact an exercise of self-mastery and a power of ethical balance, needless and impossible in older and lower states of existence.

The Buddhist doctrine of impermanency is

the doctrine also of modern science: either might be uttered in the words of the other. "Natural knowledge," wrote Huxley in one of his latest and finest essays, "tends more and more to the conclusion that 'all the choir of heaven and furniture of the earth' are the transitory forms of parcels of cosmic subtance wending along the road of evolution from nebulous potentiality, — through endless growths of sun and planet and satellite, — through all varieties of matter, — through infinite diversities of life and thought, — possibly through modes of being of which we neither have a conception nor are competent to form any, — back to the indefinable latency from which they arose. Thus the most obvious attribute of the Cosmos is its impermanency."[1]

And, finally, it may be said that Buddhism not only presents remarkable accordance with nineteenth century thought in regard to the instability of all integrations, the ethical signification of heredity, the lesson of mental evolution, the duty of moral progress, but it also agrees with science in repudiating equally

[1] *Evolution and Ethics.*

our doctrines of materialism and of spiritualism, our theory of a Creator and of special creation, and our belief in the immortality of the soul. Yet, in spite of this repudiation of the very foundations of Occidental religion, it has been able to give us the revelation of larger religious possibilities, — the suggestions of a universal scientific creed nobler than any which has ever existed. Precisely in that period of our own intellectual evolution when faith in a personal God is passing away, — when the belief in an individual soul is becoming impossible, — when the most religious minds shrink from everything that we have been calling religion, — when the universal doubt is an ever-growing weight upon ethical aspiration, — light is offered from the East. There we find ourselves in presence of an older and a vaster faith, — holding no gross anthropomorphic conceptions of the immeasurable Reality, and denying the existence of soul, but nevertheless inculcating a system of morals superior to any other, and maintaining a hope which no possible future form of positive knowledge can destroy. Reinforced by the teaching of science, the teaching of this more ancient faith is that for thousands of years we have been thinking inside-out and upside-down. The only reality is One; — all that we have taken for Substance is only Shadow; — the physical is the unreal; — *and the outer-man is the ghost.*

X

THE REBIRTH OF KATSUGORŌ

I

THE following is not a story, — at least it is not one of *my* stories. It is only the translation of an old Japanese document — or rather series of documents — very much signed and sealed, and dating back to the early part of the present century. Various authors appear to have made use of these documents: especially the compiler of the curious collection of Buddhist stories entitled *Bukkyō-hyakkwa-zenshō*, to whom they furnished the material of the twenty-sixth narrative in that work. The present translation, however, was made from a manuscript copy discovered in a private library in Tōkyō. I am responsible for nothing beyond a few notes appended to the text.

Although the beginning will probably prove dry reading, I presume to advise the perusal of the whole translation from first to last, because it suggests many things besides the possibility of remembering former births. It will be found to reflect something of the feudal Japan passed away, and something of the old-time faith, — not the higher Buddhism, but what is incomparably more difficult for any Occidental to obtain a glimpse of: the common ideas of the people concerning preëxistence and rebirth. And in view of this fact, the exactness of the official investigations, and the credibility of the evidence accepted, necessarily become questions of minor importance.

II

1. — COPY OF THE REPORT OF TAMON DEMPACHIRŌ.

The case of Katsugorō, nine years old, second son of Genzō, a farmer on my estate, dwelling in the Village called Nakanomura in the District called Tamagōri in the Province of Musashi.

Some time during the autumn of last year, the above-mentioned Katsugorō, the son of Genzō, told to his elder sister the story of his previous existence and of his rebirth. But as it seemed to be only the fancy of a child, she gave little heed to it. Afterwards, however, when Katsugorō had told her the same story over and over again, she began to think that it was a strange thing, and she told her parents about it.

During the twelfth month of the past year, Genzō himself questioned Katsugorō about the matter, whereupon Katsugorō declared, —

That he had been in his former existence the son of a certain Kyūbei, a farmer of Hodokubo-mura, which is a village within the jurisdiction of the Lord Komiya, in the district called Tamagōri, in the province of Musashi; —

That he, Katsugorō, the son of Kyūbei, had died of smallpox at the age of six years, — and

That he had been reborn thereafter into the family of the Genzō before-mentioned.

Though this seemed unbelievable, the boy repeated all the circumstances of his story with so much exactness and apparent certainty, that the Headman and the elders of the village made a formal investigation of the case. As the news of this event soon spread, it was heard by the family of a certain Hanshirō, living in the village called Hodokubo-mura; and Hanshirō then came to the house of the Genzō aforesaid, a farmer belonging to my estate, and found that everything was true which the boy had said about the personal appearance and the facial characteristics of his former parents, and about the aspect of the house which had been his home in his previous birth. Katsugorō was then taken to the house of Hanshirō in Hodokubo-mura; and the people there said that he looked very much like their Tōzō, who had died a number of years before, at the age of six. Since then the two families have been visiting each other at intervals. The people of other neighboring villages seem to have heard of the matter; and now persons come daily from various places to see Katsugorō.

A deposition regarding the above facts having been made before me by persons dwelling on my estate, I summoned the man Genzō to my house, and there examined him. His answers to my questions did not contradict the statements before-mentioned made by other parties.

Occasionally in the world some rumor of such a matter as this spreads among the people. Indeed, it is hard to believe such things. But I beg to make report of the present case, hoping the same will reach your august ear, — so that I may not be charged with negligence.

[Signed]   TAMON DEMPACHIRŌ.

The Fourth Month and the Sixth Year of Bunsei [1823].

2. — COPY OF LETTER WRITTEN BY KAZUNAWO TO TEIKIN, PRIEST OF SENGAKUJI.

I have been favored with the accompanying copy of the report of Tamon Dempachirō by Shiga Hyoëmon Sama, who brought it to me; and I take great pleasure in sending it to you. I think that it might be well for you to preserve it, together with the writing from Kwanzan Sama, which you kindly showed me the other day.

[Signed]   KAZUNAWO.

The twenty-first day of the Sixth Month. [No other date.]

3.—Copy of the Letter of Matsudaira Kwanzan [Daimyō] to the Priest Teikin of
the Temple called Sengakuji.

I herewith enclose and send you the account of the rebirth of Katsugorō. I have written it in the popular style, thinking that it might have a good effect in helping to silence those who do not believe in the doctrines of the Buddha. As a literary work it is, of course, a wretched thing. I send it to you supposing that it could only amuse you from that point of view. But as for the relation itself, it is without mistake; for I myself heard it from the grandmother of Katsugorō. When you have read it, please return it to me.

[Signed]   KWANZAN.

Twentieth day. [No date.]

[COPY.]

RELATION OF THE REBIRTH OF KATSUGORŌ.

4. — (*Introductory Note by the Priest Teikin.*)

This is the account of a true fact; for it has been written by Matsudaira Kwanzan Sama, who himself went [*to Nakano-mura*] on the twenty-second day of the third month of this year for the special purpose of inquiring about the matter.

After having obtained a glimpse of Katsugorō, he questioned the boy's grandmother as to every particular; and he wrote down her answers exactly as they were given.

Afterwards, the said Kwanzan Sama condescended to honor this temple with a visit on the fourteenth day of this fourth month, and with his own august lips told me about his visit to the family of the aforesaid Katsugorō. Furthermore, he vouchsafed me the favor of permitting me to read the before-mentioned writing, on the twentieth day of this same month. And, availing myself of the privilege, I immediately made a copy of the writing.

[Signed]   TEIKIN SŌ   Facsimile of the priest's *kakihan*, or private sign-manual, made with the brush.

Sengaku-ji

The twenty-first day of the Fourth Month of the Sixth Year of Bunsei [1823].

[COPY.]

5. — [NAMES OF THE MEMBERS OF THE TWO FAMILIES CONCERNED.]

[Family of Genzō.]

KATSUGORŌ. — Born the 10th day of the 10th month of the twelfth year of Bunkwa [1815]. Nine years old this sixth year of

Bunsei [1823].[1] Second son of Genzō, a farmer living in Tanitsuiri in Nakano-mura, district of Tamagōri, province of Musashi. — Estate of Tamon Dempachirō, whose yashiki is in the street called Shichikenchō, Nedzu, Yedo. — Jurisdiction of Yusuki.

GENZŌ. — Father of Katsugorō. Family name, Koyada. Forty-nine years old this sixth year of Bunsei. Being poor, he occupies himself with the making of baskets, which he sells in Yedo. The name of the inn at which he lodges while in Yedo is Sagamiya, kept by one Kihei, in Bakuro-chō.

SEI. — Wife of Genzō and mother of Katsugorō. Thirty-nine years old this sixth year of Bunsei. Daughter of Murata Kichitarō, samurai, — once an archer in the service of the Lord of Owari. When Sei was twelve years old she was a maid-servant, it is said, in the house of Honda Dainoshin Dono. When she was thirteen years old, her father, Kichi-

---

[1] The Western reader is requested to bear in mind that the year in which a Japanese child is born is counted always as one year in the reckoning of age.

tarō was dismissed forever for a certain cause from the service of the Lord of Owari, and he became a rōnin.[1] He died at the age of seventy-five, on the twenty-fifth day of the fourth month of the fourth year of Bunkwa [1807]. His grave is in the cemetery of the temple called Eirin-ji, of the Zen sect, in the village of Shimo-Yusuki.

TSUYA. — Grandmother of Katsugorō. Seventy-two years old this sixth year of Bunsei. When young she served as maid in the household of Matsudaira Oki-no-Kami Dono [*Daimyō*].

FUSA. — Elder sister of Katsugorō. Fifteen years old this year.

OTOJIRŌ. — Elder brother of Katsugorō. Fourteen years old this year.

TSUNÉ.—Younger sister of Katsugorō. Four years old this year.

[1] Lit.: "A wave-man," — a wandering samurai without a lord. The *rōnin* were generally a desperate and very dangerous class; but there were some fine characters among them.

[*Family of Hanshirō.*]

Tōzō. — Died at the age of six in Hodokubo-mura, in the district called Tamagōri in the province of Musashi. Estate of Nakané Uyemon, whose yashiki is in the street Atarashi-bashi-dōri, Shitaya, Yedo. Jurisdiction of Komiya. — [Tōzō] was born in the second year of Bunkwa [1805], and died at about the fourth hour of the day [*10 o'clock in the morning*] on the fourth day of the second month of the seventh year of Bunkwa [1810]. The sickness of which he died was smallpox. Buried in the graveyard on the hill above the village before-mentioned, — Hodokubo-mura. — Parochial temple: Iwōji in Misawa-mura. Sect: Zen-shū. Last year the fifth year of Bunkwa [1822], the *jiū-san kwaiki*[1] was said for Tōzō.

Hanshirō. — Stepfather of Tōzō. Family

---

[1] The Buddhist services for the dead are celebrated at regular intervals, increasing successively in length, until the time of one hundred years after death. The *jiū-san kwaiki* is the service for the thirteenth year after death. By "thirteenth" in the context the reader must understand that the year in which the death took place is counted for one year.

name: Suzaki. Fifty years old this sixth year of Bunsei.

SHIDZU. — Mother of Tōzō. Forty-nine years old this sixth year of Bunsei.

KYŪBEI (afterwards TOGŌRŌ). — Real father of Tōzō. Original name, Kyūbei, afterwards changed to Togōrō. Died at the age of forty-eight, in the sixth year of Bunkwa [1809], when Tōzō was five years old. To replace him, Hanshirō became an *iri-muko*.[1]

CHILDREN: TWO BOYS AND TWO GIRLS. — These are Hanshirō's children by the mother of Tōzō.

6. — [COPY OF THE ACCOUNT WRITTEN IN POPULAR STYLE BY MATSUDAIRA KWANZAN DONO, DAIMYŌ.]

Some time in the eleventh month of the past year, when Katsugorō was playing in the rice-field with his elder sister, Fusa, he asked her, —

[1] The second husband, by adoption, of a daughter who lives with her own parents.

"Elder Sister, where did you come from before you were born into our household?"

Fusa answered him: —

"How can I know what happened to me before I was born?"

Katsugorō looked surprised and exclaimed:

"Then you cannot remember anything that happened before you were born?"

"Do *you* remember?" asked Fusa.

"Indeed I do," replied Katsugorō. "I used to be the son of Kyūbei San of Hodokubo, and my name was then Tōzō — do you not know all that?"

"Ah!" said Fusa, "I shall tell father and mother about it."

But Katsugorō at once began to cry, and said: —

"Please do not tell! — it would not be good to tell father and mother."

Fusa made answer, after a little while: —

"Well, this time I shall not tell. But the next time that you do anything naughty, then I will tell."

After that day whenever a dispute arose between the two, the sister would threaten the brother, saying, "Very well, then — I shall tell that thing to father and mother." At these words the boy would always yield to his sister. This happened many times; and the parents one day overheard Fusa making her threat. Thinking Katsugorō must have been doing something wrong, they desired to know what the matter was, and Fusa, being questioned, told them the truth. Then Genzō and his wife, and Tsuya, the grandmother of Katsugorō, thought it a very strange thing. They called Katsugorō, therefore; and tried, first by coaxing, and then by threatening, to make him tell what he had meant by those words.

After hesitation, Katsugorō said:— "I will tell you everything. I used to be the son of Kyūbei San of Hodokubo, and the name of my mother then was O-Shidzu San. When I was five years old, Kyūbei San died; and there came in his place a man called Hanshirō San, who loved me very much. But in the following year, when I was six years old, I died of smallpox. In the third year after that I entered mother's honorable womb, and was born again."

The parents and the grandmother of the boy wondered greatly at hearing this; and they decided to make all possible inquiry as to the man called Hanshirō of Hodokubo. But as they all had to work very hard every day to earn a living, and so could spare but little time for any other matter, they could not at once carry out their intention.

Now Sei, the mother of Katsugorō, had nightly to suckle her little daughter Tsuné, who was four years old;[1] — and Katsugorō therefore slept with his grandmother, Tsuya. Sometimes he used to talk to her in bed; and one night when he was in a very confiding mood, she persuaded him to tell her what happened at the time when he had died. Then he said: — "Until I was four years old I used to remember everything; but since then I have become more and more forgetful; and now I forget many, many things. But I still remember that I died of smallpox; I remember that I was put into a jar;[2] I remember that

[1] Children in Japan, among the poorer classes, are not weaned until an age much later than what is considered the proper age for weaning children in Western countries. But "four years old" in this text may mean considerably less, than three by Western reckoning.

[2] From very ancient time in Japan it has been the custom to bury the dead in large jars, — usually of red earthenware,

THE REBIRTH OF KATSUGORO 281

I was buried on a hill. There was a hole made in the ground; and the people let the jar drop into that hole. It fell *pon!* — I remember that sound well. Then somehow I returned to the house, and I stopped on my own pillow there.[1] In a short time some old man, — looking like a grandfather — came and took me away. I do not know who or what he was. As I walked I went through empty air as if flying. I remember it was neither night nor day as we went: it was always like sunset-time. I did not feel either warm or cold or hungry. We went very far, I think; but still I could hear always, faintly, the voices of people talking at home; and the sound of the *Nembutsu* [2] being said for me.

— called *Kamé*. Such jars are still used, although a large proportion of the dead are buried in wooden coffins of a form unknown in the Occident.

[1] The idea expressed is not that of lying down with the pillow under the head, but of hovering about the pillow, or resting upon it as an insect might do. The bodiless spirit is usually said to rest upon the roof of the home. The apparition of the aged man referred to in the next sentence seems a thought of Shintō rather than of Buddhism.

[2] The repetition of the Buddhist invocation *Namu Amida Butsu!* is thus named. The *nembutsu* is repeated by many Buddhist sects besides the sect of Amida proper, — the Shinshū.

I remember also that when the people at home set offerings of hot *botamochi* [1] before the household shrine [*butsudan*], I inhaled the vapor of the offerings. . . . Grandmother, never forget to offer warm food to the honorable dead [*Hotoké Sama*], and do not forget to give to priests — I am sure it is very good to do these things.[2] . . . After that, I only remember that the old man led me by some roundabout way to this place — I remember we passed the road beyond the village. Then we came here, and he pointed to this house, and said to me: — ' Now you must be reborn, — for it is three years since you died. You are to be reborn in that house. The person who will become your grandmother is very kind; so it will be well for you to be conceived and born there.' After saying this, the old man went away. I remained a little time under the kaki-tree before the entrance of this house. Then I was going to enter

[1] *Botamochi*, a kind of sugared rice-cake.

[2] Such advice is a commonplace in Japanese Buddhist literature. By *Hotoké Sama* here the boy means, not the Buddhas proper, but the spirits of the dead, hopefully termed Buddhas by those who loved them, — much as in the West we sometimes speak of our dead as angels."

when I heard talking inside: some one said that because father was now earning so little, mother would have to go to service in Yedo. I thought, "I will not go into that house;" and I stopped three days in the garden. On the third day it was decided that, after all, mother would not have to go to Yedo. The same night I passed into the house through a knot-hole in the sliding-shutters; — and after that I stayed for three days beside the *kamado*.[1] Then I entered mother's honorable womb.[2] . . . I remember that I was born without any pain at all. — Grandmother, you may tell this to father and mother, but please never tell it to anybody else."

The grandmother told Genzō and his wife what Katsugorō had related to her; and after that the boy was not afraid to speak freely

[1] The cooking-place in a Japanese kitchen. Sometimes the word is translated "kitchen-range," but the *kamado* is something very different from a Western kitchen-range.

[2] Here I think it better to omit a couple of sentences in the original rather too plain for Western taste, yet not without interest. The meaning of the omitted passages is only that even in the womb the child acted with consideration, and according to the rules of filial piety.

with his parents on the subject of his former existence, and would often say to them: "I want to go to Hodokubo. Please let me make a visit to the tomb of Kyūbei San." Genzō thought that Katsugorō, being a strange child, would probably die before long, and that it might therefore be better to make inquiry at once as to whether there really was a man in Hodokubo called Hanshirō. But he did not wish to make the inquiry himself, because for a man to do so [*under such circumstances?*] would seem inconsiderate or forward. Therefore, instead of going himself to Hodokubo, he asked his mother Tsuya, on the twentieth day of the first month of this year, to take her grandson there.

Tsuya went with Katsugorō to Hodokubo; and when they entered the village she pointed to the nearer dwellings, and asked the boy, "Which house is it? — is it this house or that one?" "No," answered Katsugorō, — "it is further on — much further," — and he hurried before her. Reaching a certain dwelling at last, he cried, "This is the house!" — and ran in, without waiting for his grandmother. Tsuya followed him in, and asked the people

THE REBIRTH OF KATSUGORO 285

there what was the name of the owner of the house. "Hanshirō," one of them answered. She asked the name of Hanshirō's wife. "Shidzu," was the reply. Then she asked whether there had ever been a son called Tōzō born in that house. "Yes," was the answer; "but that boy died thirteen years ago, when he was six years old."

Then for the first time Tsuya was convinced that Katsugorō had spoken the truth; and she could not help shedding tears. She related to the people of the house all that Katsugorō had told her about his remembrance of his former birth. Then Hanshirō and his wife wondered greatly. They caressed Katsugorō and wept; and they remarked that he was much handsomer now than he had been as Tōzō before dying at the age of six. In the mean time, Katsugorō was looking all about; and seeing the roof of a tobacco shop opposite to the house of Hanshirō, he pointed to it, and said: — "That used not to be there." And he also said, — "The tree yonder used not to be there." All this was true. So from the minds of Hanshirō and his wife every doubt departed [*ga wo orishi*].

On the same day Tsuya and Katsugorō returned to Tanitsuiri, Nakano-mura. Afterwards Genzō sent his son several times to Hanshirō's house, and allowed him to visit the tomb of Kyūbei his real father in his previous existence.

Sometimes Katsugorō says:—"I am a *Nono-Sama:*[1] therefore please be kind to me." Sometimes he also says to his grandmother:—"I think I shall die when I am sixteen; but, as Ontaké Sama[2] has taught us,

---

[1] *Nono-San* (or *Sama*) is the child-word for the Spirits of the dead, for the Buddhas, and for the Shintō Gods,— Kami. *Nono-San wo ogamu,*—"to pray to the Nono-San," is the child-phrase for praying to the gods. The spirits of the ancestors become Nono-San,—*Kami,*—according to Shintō thought.

[2] The reference here to Ontaké Sama has a particular interest, but will need some considerable explanation.

Ontaké, or Mitaké, is the name of a celebrated holy peak in the province of Shinano—a great resort for pilgrims. During the Tokugawa Shōgunate, a priest called Isshin, of the Risshū Buddhists, made a pilgrimage to that mountain. Returning to his native place (Sakamoto-chō, Shitaya, Yedo), he began to preach certain new doctrines, and to make for himself a reputation as a miracle-worker, by virtue of powers said to have been gained during his pilgrimage to Ontaké. The Shōgunate considered him a dangerous person, and banished him to the island of Hachijō,

dying is not a matter to be afraid of." When his parents ask him, "Would you not like to become a priest?" he answers, "I would rather not be a priest."

where he remained for some years. Afterwards he was allowed to return to Yedo, and there to preach his new faith, — to which he gave the name of Azuma-Kyō. It was Buddhist teaching in a Shintō disguise, — the deities especially adored by its followers being Okuni-nushi and Sukuna-hikona as Buddhist avatars. In the prayer of the sect called Kaibyaku-Norito it is said: — "The divine nature is immovable (*fudō*); yet it moves. It is formless, yet manifests itself in forms. This is the Incomprehensible Divine Body. In Heaven and Earth it is called Kami; in all things it is called Spirit; in Man it is called Mind. . . . From this only reality came the heavens, the four oceans, the great whole of the three thousand universes; — from the One Mind emanate three thousands of great thousands of forms." . . .

In the eleventh year of Bunkwa (1814) a man called Shimoyama Osuké, originally an oil-merchant in Heiyemon-chō, Asakusa, Yedo, organized, on the basis of Isshin's teaching, a religious association named Tomoyé-Ko. It flourished until the overthrow of the Shōgunate, when a law was issued forbidding the teaching of mixed doctrines, and the blending of Shintō with Buddhist religion. Shimoyama Osuké then applied for permission to establish a new Shintō sect, under the name of Mitaké-Kyō, — popularly called Ontaké-Kyō; and the permission was given in the sixth year of Meiji [1873]. Osuké then remodeled the Buddhist sutra *Fudō Kyō* into a Shintō prayer-book, under

The village people do not call him Katsugorō any more; they have nicknamed him "Hodokubo-Kozō" (the Acolyte of Hodokubo).[1] When any one visits the house to see him, he becomes shy at once, and runs to hide himself in the inner apartments. So it is not possible to have any direct conversation with him. I have written down this account exactly as his grandmother gave it to me.

I asked whether Genzō, his wife, or Tsuya, could any of them remember having done any

---

the title, Shintō-Fudō-Norito. The sect still flourishes; and one of its chief temples is situated about a mile from my present residence in Tōkyō.

"Ontaké San" (or "Sama") is a popular name given to the deities adored by this sect. It really means the Deity dwelling on the peak Mitaké, or Ontaké. But the name is also sometimes applied to the high-priest of the sect, who is supposed to be oracularly inspired by the deity of Ontaké, and to make revelations of truth through the power of the divinity. In the mouth of the boy Katsugorō "Ontaké Sama" means the high-priest of that time [1823], almost certainly Osuké himself, — then chief of the Tomoyé-Kyō.

[1] *Kozō* is the name given to a Buddhist acolyte, or a youth studying for the priesthood. But it is also given to errand-boys and little boy-servants sometimes, — perhaps because in former days the heads of little boys were shaved. I think that the meaning in this text is "acolyte."

virtuous deeds. Genzō and his wife said that they had never done anything especially virtuous; but that Tsuya, the grandmother, had always been in the habit of repeating the *Nembutsu* every morning and evening, and that she never failed to give two *mon*[1] to any priest or pilgrim who came to the door. But excepting these small matters, she never had done anything which could be called a particularly virtuous act.

(— *This is the End of the Relation of the Rebirth of Katsugorō.*)

7. — (NOTE BY THE TRANSLATOR.)

The foregoing is taken from a manuscript entitled *Chin Setsu Shū Ki;* or, "Manuscript-Collection of Uncommon Stories," — made between the fourth month of the sixth year of Bunsei and the tenth month of the sixth year of Tempō [1823–1835]. At the end of the manuscript is written, — "*From the years of Bunsei to the years of Tempō.* — *Minamisempa, Owner: Kurumachō, Shiba,*

[1] In that time the name of the smallest of coins = $\frac{1}{10}$ of 1 cent. It was about the same as that now called *rin*, a copper with a square hole in the middle and bearing Chinese characters.

Yedo." Under this, again, is the following note: — "*Bought from Yamatoya Sakujirō Nishinokubo: twenty-first day* [?], *Second Year of Meiji* [1869]." From which it would appear that the manuscript had been written by Minamisempa, who collected stories told to him, or copied them from manuscripts obtained by him, during the thirteen years from 1823 to 1835, inclusive.

III

Perhaps somebody will now be unreasonable enough to ask whether I believe this story, — as if my belief or disbelief had anything to do with the matter! The question of the possibility of remembering former births seems to me to depend upon the question what it is that remembers. If it is the Infinite All-Self in each one of us, then I can believe the whole of the *Jatakas* without any trouble. As to the False Self, the mere woof and warp of sensation and desire, then I can best express my idea by relating a dream which I once dreamed. Whether it was a dream of the night or a dream of the day need not concern any one, — since it was only a dream.

XI

WITHIN THE CIRCLE

Neither personal pain nor personal pleasure can be really expressed in words. It is never possible to communicate them in their original form. It is only possible, by vivid portrayal of the circumstances or conditions causing them, to awaken in sympathetic minds some kindred qualities of feeling. But if the circumstances causing the pain or the pleasure be totally foreign to common human experience, then no representation of them can make fully known the sensations which they evoked. Hopeless, therefore, any attempt to tell the real pain of seeing my former births. I can say only that no combination of suffering possible to *individual* being could be likened to such pain, — the pain of countless lives interwoven. It seemed as if every nerve of me had been prolonged into some monstrous web of sentiency spun back through a million years, — and as if the whole of that measureless woof and warp, over all its shivering threads, were pouring into my consciousness, out of the abysmal past, some ghastliness without name, — some horror too vast for human brain to hold. For, as I looked backward, I became double, quadruple, octuple; — I multiplied by arithmetical progression; — I became hundreds and thousands, — and feared with the terror of thousands, — and despaired with the anguish of thousands, — and shuddered with the agony of thousands; yet knew the pleasure of none. All joys, all delights appeared but mists or mockeries: only the pain and the fear were real, — and always, always growing. Then in the moment when sentiency itself seemed bursting into dissolution, one divine touch ended the frightful vision, and brought again to me the simple consciousness of the single present. Oh! how unspeakably delicious that sudden shrinking back out of multiplicity into unity! — that immense, immeasurable collapse of Self into the blind oblivious numbness of individuality!

"To others also," said the voice of the divine

one who had thus saved me, — "to others in the like state it has been permitted to see something of their prëexistence. But no one of them ever could endure to look far. Power to see all former births belongs only to those eternally released from the bonds of Self. Such exist outside of illusion, — outside of form and name; and pain cannot come nigh them.

"But to you, remaining in illusion, not even the Buddha could give power to look back more than a little way.

"Still you are bewitched by the follies of art and of poetry and of music, — the delusions of color and form, — the delusions of sensuous speech, the delusions of sensuous sound.

"Still that apparition called Nature — which is but another name for emptiness and shadow — deceives and charms you, and fills you with dreams of longing for the things of sense.

"But he who truly wishes to know, must not love this phantom Nature, — must not find delight in the radiance of a clear sky, — nor in the sight of the sea, — nor in the sound of the flowing of rivers, — nor in the forms of peaks and woods and valleys, — nor in the colors of them.

"He who truly wishes to know must not find delight in contemplating the works and the deeds of men, nor in hearing their converse, nor in observing the puppet-play of their passions and of their emotions. All this is but a weaving of smoke, — a shimmering of vapors, — an impermanency, — a phantasmagory.

"For the pleasures that men term lofty or noble or sublime are but larger sensualisms, subtler falsities: venomous fair-seeming flowerings of selfishness, — all rooted in the elder slime of appetites and desires. To joy in the radiance of a cloudless day, — to see the mountains shift their tintings to the wheeling of the sun, — to watch the passing of waves, the fading of sunsets, — to find charm in the blossoming of plants or trees: all this is of the senses. Not less truly of the senses is the pleasure of observing actions called great or beautiful or heroic, — since it is one with the pleasure of imagining those things for which men miserably strive in this miserable world: brief love and fame and honor, — all of which are empty as passing foam.

"Sky, sun, and sea; — the peaks, the

woods, the plains; — all splendors and forms and colors, — are spectres. The feelings and the thoughts and the acts of men, — whether deemed high or low, noble or ignoble, — all things imagined or done for any save the eternal purpose, are but dreams born of dreams and begetting hollowness. To the clear of sight, all feelings of self, — all love and hate, joy and pain, hope and regret, are alike shadows; — youth and age, beauty and horror, sweetness and foulness, are not different; — death and life are one and the same; and Space and Time exist but as the stage and the order of the perpetual Shadow-play.

"All that exists in Time must perish. To the Awakened there is no Time or Space or Change, — no night or day, — no heat or cold, — no moon or season, — no present, past, or future. Form and the names of form are alike nothingness: — Knowledge only is real; and unto whomsoever gains it, the universe becomes a ghost. But it is written: — '*He who hath overcome Time in the past and the future must be of exceedingly pure understanding.*'

"Such understanding is not yours. Still

to your eyes the shadow seems the substance, — and darkness, light, — and voidness, beauty. And therefore to see your former births could give you only pain."

I asked: —

"Had I found strength to look back to the beginning, — back to the verge of Time, — could I have read the Secret of the universe?"

"Nay," was answer made. "Only by Infinite Vision can the Secret be read. Could you have looked back incomparably further than your power permitted, then the Past would have become for you the Future. And could you have endured even yet more, the Future would have orbed back for you into the Present."

"Yet why?" I murmured, marveling. . . . "What is the Circle?"

"Circle there is none," was the response; — "Circle there is none but the great phantom-whirl of birth and death to which, by their own thoughts and deeds, the ignorant remain condemned. But this has being only in Time; and Time itself is illusion."

Other TUT BOOKS available:

BACHELOR'S HAWAII *by Boye de Mente*

BACHELOR'S JAPAN *by Boye de Mente*

BACHELOR'S MEXICO *by Boye de Mente*

A BOOK OF NEW ENGLAND LEGENDS AND FOLK LORE *by Samuel Adams Drake*

THE BUDDHA TREE *by Fumio Niwa; translated by Kenneth Strong*

CALABASHES AND KINGS: An Introduction to Hawaii *by Stanley D. Porteus*

CHINA COLLECTING IN AMERICA *by Alice Morse Earle*

CHINESE COOKING MADE EASY *by Rosy Tseng*

CHOI OI!: The Lighter Side of Vietnam *by Tony Zidek*

CONFUCIUS SAY *by Leo Shaw*

THE COUNTERFEITER and Other Stories *by Yasushi Inoue; translated by Leon Picon*

CURIOUS PUNISHMENTS OF BYGONE DAYS *by Alice Morse Earle*

CUSTOMS AND FASHIONS IN OLD NEW ENGLAND *by Alice Morse Earle*

DINING IN SPAIN *by Gerrie Beene and Lourdes Miranda King*

EXOTICS AND RETROSPECTIVES *by Lafcadio Hearn*

FIRST YOU TAKE A LEEK: A Guide to Elegant Eating Spiced with Culinary Capers *by Maxine J. Saltonstall*

FIVE WOMEN WHO LOVED LOVE *by Saikaku Ihara; translated by William Theodore de Bary*

A FLOWER DOES NOT TALK: Zen Essays *by Abbot Zenkei Shibayama of the Nanzenji*

FOLK LEGENDS OF JAPAN *by Richard M. Dorson*

GLEANINGS IN BUDDHA-FIELDS: Studies of Hand and Soul in the Far East *by Lafcadio Hearn*

GOING NATIVE IN HAWAII: A Poor Man's Guide to Paradise *by Timothy Head*

HAIKU IN ENGLISH *by Harold G. Henderson*

HARP OF BURMA *by Michio Takeyama; translated by Howard Hibbett*

THE HAWAIIAN GUIDE BOOK for Travelers *by Henry M. Whitney*

HAWAII: End of the Rainbow *by Kazuo Miyamoto*

HAWAIIAN PHRASE BOOK

HISTORIC MANSIONS AND HIGHWAYS AROUND BOSTON *by Samuel Adams Drake*

HISTORICAL AND GEOGRAPHICAL DICTIONARY OF JAPAN *by E. Papinot*

A HISTORY OF JAPANESE LITERATURE *by W. G. Aston*

HOMEMADE ICE CREAM AND SHERBERT *by Sheila MacNiven Cameron*

HOW TO READ CHARACTER: A New Illustrated Handbook of Phrenology and Physiognomy, for Students and Examiners *by Samuel R. Wells*

IN GHOSTLY JAPAN *by Lafcadio Hearn*

INDIAN RIBALDRY *by Randor Guy*

JAPAN: An Attempt at Interpretation *by Lafcadio Hearn*

THE JAPANESE ABACUS *by Takashi Kojima*

THE JAPANESE ARE LIKE THAT *by Ichiro Kawasaki*

JAPANESE ETIQUETTE: An Introduction *by the World Fellowship Committee of the Tokyo Y.W.C.A.*

THE JAPANESE FAIRY BOOK *compiled by Yei Theodora Ozaki*

JAPANESE FOLK-PLAYS: The Ink-Smeared Lady and Other Kyogen *translated by Shio Sakanishi*

JAPANESE FOOD AND COOKING *by Stuart Griffin*

JAPANESE HOMES AND THIER SURROUNDINGS *by Edward S. Morse*

A JAPANESE MISCELLANY *by Lafcadio Hearn*

JAPANESE RECIPES *by Tatsuji Tada*

JAPANESE TALES OF MYSTERY & IMAGINATION *by Edogawa Rampo; translated by James B. Harris*

JAPANESE THINGS: Being Notes on Various Subjects Connected with Japan *by Basil Hall Chamberlain*

THE JOKE'S ON JUDO *by Donn Draeger and Ken Tremayne*

THE KABUKI HANDBOOK *by Aubrey S. Halford and Giovanna M. Halford*

KAPPA *by Ryūnosuke Akutagawa; translated by Geoffrey Bownas*

KOKORO: Hints and Echoes of Japanese Inner Life *by Lafcadio Hearn*

KOREAN FOLK TALES *by Im Bang and Yi Ryuk; translated by James S. Gale*

KOTTŌ: Being Japanese Curios, with Sundry Cobwebs *by Lafcadio Hearn*

KWAIDAN: Stories and Studies of Strange Things *by Lafcadio Hearn*

LET'S STUDY JAPANESE *by Jun Maeda*

THE LIFE OF BUDDHA *by A. Ferdinand Herold*

MODERN JAPANESE PRINTS: A Contemporary Selection *edited by Yuji Abe*

MORE ZILCH: The Marine Corps' Most Guarded Secret *by Roy Delgado*

NIHONGI: Chronicles of Japan from the Earliest Times to A.D. 697 *by W. G. Aston*

OLD LANDMARKS AND HISTORIC PERSONAGES OF BOSTON *by Samuel Adams Drake*

ORIENTAL FORTUNE TELLING *by Jimmei Shimano; translated by Togo Taguchi*

PHYSICAL FITNESS: A Practical Program *by Clark Hatch*

POO POO MAKE PRANT GLOW *by Harvey Ward*

PROFILES OF MODERN AMERICAN AUTHORS *by Bernard Dekle*

READ JAPANESE TODAY *by Len Walsh*

SELF DEFENSE SIMPLIFIED IN PICTURES *by Don Hepler*

SHADOWINGS *by Lafcadio Hearn*

A SHORT SYNOPSIS OF THE MOST ESSENTIAL POINTS IN HAWAIIAN GRAMMAR *by W. D. Alexander*

THE STORY BAG: A Collection of Korean Folk Tales *by Kim So-un; translated by Setsu Higashi*

SUMI-E: An Introduction to Ink Painting *by Nanae Momiyama*

SUN-DIALS AND ROSES OF YESTERDAY *by Alice Morse Earle*

THE TEN FOOT SQUARE HUT AND TALES OF THE HEIKE: Being Two Thirteenth-century Japanese classics, the "Hojoki" and selections from the "Heike Monogatari" *translated by A. L. Sadler*

THIS SCORCHING EARTH *by Donald Richie*

TIMES-SQUARE SAMURAI or the Improbable Japanese Occupation of New York *by Robert B. Johnson and Billie Niles Chadbourne*

TO LIVE IN JAPAN *by Mary Lee O'Neal and Virginia Woodruff*

THE TOURIST AND THE REAL JAPAN *by Boye de Mente*

TOURS OF OKINAWA: A Souvenir Guide to Places of Interest *compiled by Gasei Higa, Isamu Fuchaku, and Zenkichi Toyama*

TWO CENTURIES OF COSTUME IN AMERICA *by Alice Morse Earle*

TYPHOON! TYPHOON! An Illustrated Haiku Sequence *by Lucile M. Bogue*

UNBEATEN TRACKS IN JAPAN: An Account of Travels in the Interior Including Visits to the Aborigines of Yezo and the Shrine of Nikko *by Isabella L. Bird*

ZILCH! The Marine Corps' Most Guarded Secret *by Roy Delgado*

Please order from your bookstore or write directly to:

CHARLES E. TUTTLE CO., INC.
Suido 1-chome, 2-6, Bunkyo-ku, Tokyo 112

or:

CHARLES E. TUTTLE CO., INC.
Rutland, Vermont 05701 U.S.A.